High Seas Wranglers

Wild Florida

UNIVERSITY PRESS OF FLORIDA

Florida A&M University, Tallahassee
Florida Atlantic University, Boca Raton
Florida Gulf Coast University, Ft. Myers
Florida International University, Miami
Florida State University, Tallahassee
New College of Florida, Sarasota
University of Central Florida, Orlando
University of Florida, Gainesville
University of North Florida, Jacksonville
University of South Florida, Tampa
University of West Florida, Pensacola

UNIVERSITY PRESS OF FLORIDA

Gainesville · Tallahassee · Tampa · Boca Raton · Pensacola · Orlando · Miami · Jacksonville · Ft. Myers · Sarasota

High Seas Wranglers

The Lives of Atlantic Fishing Captains

TERRY L. HOWARD

VIVA FLORIDA 500
1513-2013

A Florida Quincentennial Book

Frontispiece: Creative Commons licensed Flickr photo shared by Repoort.

Printed in the United States of America. This book is printed on Glatfelter Natures Book, a paper certified under the standards of the Forestry Stewardship Council (FSC). It is a recycled stock that contains 30 percent post-consumer waste and is acid free.

This book may be available in an electronic edition.

18 17 16 15 14 13   6 5 4 3 2 1

A record of cataloging-in-publication data is available from the Library of Congress.
ISBN 978-0-8130-4496-5

The University Press of Florida is the scholarly publishing agency for the State University System of Florida, comprising Florida A&M University, Florida Atlantic University, Florida Gulf Coast University, Florida International University, Florida State University, New College of Florida, University of Central Florida, University of Florida, University of North Florida, University of South Florida, and University of West Florida.

University Press of Florida
15 Northwest 15th Street
Gainesville, FL 32611-2079
http://www.upf.com

For A. J. Brown

As the sun rises in the Atlantic east of Fort Pierce, Florida, another day of fishing begins.

You did not kill the fish only to keep alive and to sell for food, he thought. You killed him for pride and because you are a fisherman.

Ernest Hemingway, *The Old Man and the Sea*

Contents

Introduction 1

1. **CAPTAIN TRIS COLKET** 9

2. **CAPTAIN A. J. BROWN** 55

3. **CAPTAIN RAY PEREZ** 83

4. **CAPTAIN GLENN CAMERON** 109

5. **CAPTAIN GEORGE KAUL** 137

Conclusion 179

Glossary 183

Acknowledgments 187

Index 189

Terry Howard and Dan Darrisaw mackerel fishing in the Fort Pierce Inlet in Howard's boat, *Miss Fannie*. Photo by Jean Ann Gray.

Introduction

Blind luck, sir, and that's the God's honest. Take it from a ship's brat what knows, as they say. It's always a matter of blind luck for men like us. As long as God loves fools and the fishing is good we go on. As for my boat, it would be fair and honest to say we found each other, but isn't that always the way of it, sir? Like true love, every now and then a fellow gets lucky, don't you know.

Thomas Steinbeck, *Down to a Soundless Sea*

High Seas Wranglers: The Lives of Atlantic Fishing Captains chronicles the lives and experiences of five extraordinary Florida fishing captains. They are among the current generation of fishermen, and each is highly respected for his skill and competence. Two are Vietnam War veterans, and one is a veteran of Fidel Castro's Revolution. They live in and fish out of Fort Pierce, a town with a rich fishing history that was once billed as "The Fishing Capital of the World."

These men have unique pasts and have followed various avenues to become great Atlantic fishing captains. If there is a common theme, it is that each had an early affinity for the sea and boats and a love of fishing. Their stories, told in their own words, are filled with adventure, excitement, and intrigue. They also provide rare and valuable insights into the history of Florida's commercial and charter fishing industries.

Three of the captains are commercial hook-and-line king mackerel fishermen, and two are ocean charter captains. Commercial hook-and-line king mackerel troll fishing is very different from ocean charter fishing. A common misconception is that commercial captains take people out fishing. They do not. Charter captains take paying clients fishing; commercial hook-and-line king mackerel captains are usually not licensed to take people aboard their boats on recreational charters. Although some commercial captains maintain charter licenses and some charter captains maintain commercial licenses, most concentrate on only one of those two types of fishing. Commercial fishermen are paid for the fish they sell; charter captains are paid by the clients they take fishing. Most commercial hook-and-liners prefer to fish alone.

Commercial hook-and-line king mackerel captains do not use fishing poles or nets, which is another common misconception. They troll for fish, pulling one fish in at a time, by hand with hand lines attached to outriggers. These lines usually consist of thirty to forty feet of stainless steel aircraft cable that connects the outrigger lines to 12-, 14-, 16-, or 24-ounce planers (also called paravanes).

The size of the planer depends on the preference of the fisherman. The type and length of the lines behind the planers also vary with each fisherman. Some use all monofilament line, while others use part mono and part #8 or #9 piano wire connected by a swivel.

The lengths of these lines vary, too, though they are normally between 100 feet and 150 feet. The common bait tied on the end of these lines is a #3½ or #4 Drone spoon or a sea witch with two hooks and a carefully cut piece of strip bait. Strip baits are mostly mullet or pogies (menhaden).

All of these lines—the cable, the planer, and the monofilament and/or wire—are piled neatly on the deck at the fisherman's feet as the fish are being pulled into the boat. This line must be piled in such a way that it feeds back out quickly and cleanly in order to catch the next fish. It's very important that the fisherman not be standing in or get tangled in this pile of line. If a porpoise or a large shark should take the fish that is being pulled in, the line might fly out of the boat as if it were hooked to a passing freight train. This is a very real danger, especially in waters off of Fort Pierce, where porpoises are unusually prevalent.

Once a fish is pulled into the boat, it is unhooked on an H-shaped dehooker mounted above the "kill box" into which the fish falls. Shortly thereafter the fish is gutted and packed in ice, thus ensuring a quality product.

Commercial fishermen can steer their boats from a helm or tiller in the stern. This is the work area, where they cut bait, bait hooks, retie hooks or spoons, land fish, and adjust their position over drops or ledges, reefs, or schools of fish. Also located in the stern is a switch for operating an electric reel. These reels hold 200–300 feet of #8 or #9 stainless steel piano wire tied at the base of the reel to a barrel swivel and a length of heavy monofilament line. This wire line is baited with a sea witch and strip bait—in which case it is called a float line—or a feathered hook called a jerk bug, which the fisherman pulls or jerks continually to attract fish.

It is always a thrill to have a fish strike this bug line—especially a big fish in the twenty- to thirty-pound range or over. When they bite while your hand is pulling on this line, it feels like you've snagged the bottom.

For unknown reasons, sometimes the fish bite only on the bug- or jerk line attached to the electric reel, and sometimes they bite only on the hand lines attached to the boat's outriggers. When fishing is hot, fish bite on both; that's when it's really fun and exciting. It is not uncommon to work oneself into a sweat pulling fish when the fishing is furious.

Fishermen live for these times. Highly skilled commercial fishermen, like those interviewed in this book, handle these operations with great dexterity. Like rodeo professionals, who rope and wrestle calves, commercial kingfishermen are adept at landing fish quickly and efficiently with a minimum of effort and with few tangles or screwups. Often a bite of fish may only last for a short period of time—an hour or two—so those fishermen who have the fewest problems during the bite will catch the most.

While commercial kingfishermen primarily target king mackerel, they often hook bycatches of other species. Most common are barracuda and bonito (little tuna), which have little monetary value. Sometimes the fish houses will not even buy barracuda or bonito. Rarer, but far more lucrative, bycatches are dolphin (mahimahi), cobia, tuna, and wahoo.

When kingfishing is poor, commercial hand-line boats fish near the beach for Spanish mackerel, which are not as valuable as king mackerel but are generally more bountiful.

Bycatches of jack crevalles and bluefish are often, but not always, mixed in with the Spanish mackerel.

Experienced kingfishermen can often identify a species by how it pulls and fights on the line. They hate hooking bonito, because they pull so hard, and they blast back and forth behind the boat, often tangling other lines. Fishermen call bonito "arm stretchers," and they are seldom worth much, maybe 20–30 cents a pound. Barracuda, even large ones, feel like they are planing or gliding to the boat more easily than a king mackerel, which, if allowed, will pull and gyrate feverishly.

It's best to pull a fish smoothly and steadily to the boat without letting it turn its head, thus allowing it to do most of its fighting in the boat's kill box. Once a large fish knows it can turn its head and change directions, it is difficult to get it pulling straight again. And once any fish sees the stern of the boat and sizes up the situation, it generally goes wild. Most experienced charter captains can also identify a hooked species by how it pulls and fights on the line and pole.

On Florida's east coast two groups of king mackerel are identified from past fish-tagging programs carried out by the National Marine Fisheries Services (NMFS). The Atlantic Group, or winter stock, is believed to migrate south from the North Atlantic, and the Gulf Group, or summer stock, is thought to migrate here from the Gulf of Mexico. Annual total-allowable-catch (TAC) quotas for each group are set by the NMFS. From April 1 to October 31, commercial kingfishermen on the east coast of Florida are allowed a seventy-five-head daily trip limit of kingfish from the summer stock. A fifty-head daily trip limit is allowed from November 1 until March 31 for the winter stock. Once the TAC quota for either of these stocks of fish is met, the fishery is closed. These are the king mackerel vessel trip limits only for the Exclusive Economic Zone (EEZ) between Florida's Volusia and Monroe Counties. To further complicate matters, there are many other EEZs along the east coast of the United States and the Gulf of Mexico with different total allowable catches and daily trip limits. Though complicated, these regulations are in place to ensure a perpetual supply of king mackerel.

Today, fishermen must also provide the NMFS with detailed daily logs that include a variety of specific data, such as pounds of each species caught; depth of the water where they were caught; amount of fuel used; cost of the fuel, tackle, ice, groceries, and other supplies; and amount of bait used or discarded. These regulations are the bane of commercial fishermen and have caused some to quit.

When I began as a commercial fisherman in 1978, all I needed was a Florida Commercial Salt Water Products license, which required a $25 fee. Several state and federal licenses are required today, each with different requirements, fees, and proof-of-catch history. Times have changed. Of course, when I began commercial fishing, there were few rules, and huge net boats were slaughtering massive schools of king mackerel with impunity.

Commercial fishermen have income only when they catch and sell fish. During hard times—when winds are high and boats cannot enter the ocean or when fishing is poor—commercial fishermen have no earnings. Many have other vocational abilities, like carpentry, or mechanical skills to help supplement their fishing income. Many also rely on working wives during slow times.

Successful commercial fishermen have many talents. Not only are they captains, but they are also mates, mechanics, fiberglass and wood specialists, and navigators. Boats, engines, and equipment require a great deal of upkeep. Most take great pride in their skills, all of which contribute to their success as commercial kingfish captains.

In order to maintain their business and boats, charter captains must also have a host of skills and talents. Plus, they are also responsible for the clients they carry out on the ocean. Charter captains make their money before they leave the dock. Because their boats are usually larger, with more powerful engines, they can fish in higher seas, though sometimes they must, reluctantly, return the clients' fees if weather or fishing is deemed too poor.

Charter captains cater to the wishes of their clients, with an eye on how best to serve them. Experienced fishing clients might be able to handle rough weather and seas better than a family with no ocean experience. Captains might suggest that the latter wait for better conditions. Sailfish or marlin are the most popular target fish for charters. Inexperienced ocean clients are usually excited to catch a barracuda or a bonito, both of which provide a challenging fight on rod and reel. Kingfish, which give clients meat to take home, are another popular staple for charters. Dolphin (mahimahi), wahoo, and cobia, like kingfish, are also desirable because of their food value as well as their fighting ability. When large manta rays migrate up the Florida coast, they are often followed by cobia, which like to swim in the shade of the large rays' wings. Wahoo are more difficult to target because their patterns are less predictable.

Charter captains also drift or anchor over wrecks and reefs for red snapper, grouper, and sea bass; however, recent lengthy closures on these species have curtailed the bottom-fishing aspect of the business.

When snapper, grouper, and sea bass are not available, captains often target large amberjacks. Amberjack meat is not as tasty as grouper or snapper, but it is good, and they are great fighters.

Success for both charter and commercial captains is predicated entirely on their skill in maintaining their boat, equipment, and tackle, as well as on knowing where, when, and how to fish. Those who consistently do everything right have the best catches. Competent captains are looked up to and highly respected in many circles, but especially on the waterfront.

While all of the captains in this book reside in Fort Pierce, Florida, they travel up and down the Atlantic coast and, in the case of the charter captains, to the Bahamas and other countries in the Caribbean and Gulf of Mexico. Fort Pierce, located about halfway down the Florida peninsula, provides a central base from which to travel. The east coast of Florida is bordered by a barrier island with several cuts or inlets through it to the Atlantic. Along with its central location Fort Pierce has arguably the widest and safest inlet on Florida's Atlantic coast. Though fishing here is not as good as it once was, it is still excellent. In the fishing grounds off the Fort Pierce Inlet, as in the waters off all inlets, are many rocks, wrecks, and reefs known to the fishermen. The area along the beach itself is known for large kingfish, or smokers.

Approximately ten miles east of the Fort Pierce Inlet is the western edge of the Gulf Stream, a warm ocean current that originates in the Gulf of Mexico, flows eastward through the Florida Straits, and then travels north along the east coast of the United States. Its western edge flows near the beach in Miami, Florida, three to five miles out in the Palm Beaches, twenty to thirty miles east of Cape Canaveral, and nearly fifty miles offshore near Jacksonville, Florida. As the Gulf Stream flows north its edge is gradually farther off of North America. By the time the current reaches Newfoundland it is flowing east toward Europe. Early explorers would ride the current from the New World back to Europe, even with unfavorable winds. The western edge of this warm ocean current has always been a rich fishing ground, especially off the east coast of Florida.

The offshore bar near Fort Pierce is an intermittent reef that runs north and south off of St. Lucie County in about ninety feet of water. An inshore bar runs mostly parallel to this in about seventy-five feet of water. The inshore and offshore bars run from southeast of the Fort Pierce Inlet to about twenty miles north-northeast, to where the Bethel Shoals Buoy is located. During World War II, German U-boats would navigate to the light at this buoy, because the Bethel Buoy was shown on all of their charts. They would lie on the bottom during the day and surface at night to sink Allied ships passing along the coast in the shipping lanes.

North of the Bethel Shoals Buoy is the south end of the Sebastian, Florida, fishing grounds. The Sebastian Inlet is located in Indian River County and is the next inlet to the north of Fort Pierce. Its fishing grounds extend north twenty to thirty miles, to the area off Cape Canaveral. Often during winter months, east coast king mackerel boats fish out of Sebastian or the Cape because the kingfishing is better there. And, at times, in the spring and summer, large schools of kingfish show up south of Fort Pierce, near Jupiter and the Palm Beaches, and many commercial kingfish captains follow.

With the possible exception of commercial troll salmon boats in the northeastern and northwestern parts of the United States, commercial hand-line troll kingfishing is arguably the most ecologically sound form of commercial fishing today. Fish often simply do not bite, thus naturally preserving themselves. Undersized fish and species that fishermen are prohibited from catching are released unharmed. Caught fish are quickly gutted and packed on ice. With carefully monitored total-allowable-catch limits and daily trip limits of fifty or seventy-five head of fish per boat, the sustainability of king mackerel populations can be assured.

The commercial hand-line fishermen of the EEZ on the east coast of Florida wish that all EEZs had the same daily trip limits. Unfortunately, other EEZs (notably, those north of Volusia County and south of Dade County and into the Gulf of Mexico) have much higher individual daily catch limits—1,250 to 3,500 pounds—which can negatively impact large migrating schools of fish. Hand-line commercial kingfishermen are conservationists. They are very much in favor of the sustainability of all of the ocean's species, and especially king and Spanish mackerel.

Today's charter captains are also strong proponents of species sustainability. All I have known encourage their clients to keep only what they will eat and release all other fish. They also take careful measurements of trophy fish before releasing them alive. That way, plastic models or replicas of the fish can be made for mounting on the fisherman's walls; the days of a taxidermist's stuffing or mounting the actual fish are all but over. Commercial and charter captains know well that the only way to maintain their unique way of life is to preserve the ocean's bounty.

It is my hope that the reader will be introduced to and enlightened by the wonderful, and rapidly declining, way of life that is depicted in the stories shared by these exceptional Atlantic fishing captains. This book is filled with rich Florida history, fishing tales, war stories, tragedies and near-tragedies, daring rescues, and sea adventures. It is also my wish that the reader derive as much enjoyment reading these tales as I did collecting them. It has been a pleasure and honor to chronicle the amazing lives of these men.

1

Captain Tris Colket

Captain Tris Colket (Tristram Coffin Colket IV) is passionate about the sea, fishing, and his boat, *Last Mango*. After earning his bachelor's degree from Rollins College in Winter Park, Florida, Tris came back to the Indian River area, where he had grown up, and found that he could make a living doing what he loved most—fishing. He never looked back. He has been a successful hand-line king mackerel fisherman, a swordfisherman, a tilefisherman, a shark fisherman, and he is currently a charter captain.

Tris Colket's vast understanding of the ocean and its bounty comes from more than forty years in commercial and charter fishing. He has participated in nearly every kind of ocean hook-and-line fishery. Few people today can match his knowledge of east coast commercial fishing, especially of sharks and their habits. And few can match his overall experience on the ocean.

Tris told me he comes from a long line of adventurers. His great-grandfather once made arrangements to stay at a hotel in Cairo, Egypt, giving as his home address King of Prussia, Pennsylvania. When he and his party arrived in Cairo, Tris said that they received the red-carpet treatment, and no expense was spared by the hotel staff, which was expecting the King of Prussia.

Tris's many stories and adventures include tense boardings by Coast Guard and other law-enforcement agencies, daring sea rescues, capturing and transporting live sharks for Sea World, collaborating with the world's leading shark experts, and experiencing frightening weather conditions, including one particularly terrifying stormy night at sea. Today, Tris Colket is a leading Fort Pierce charter captain. Though his charter business is relatively new, it is flourishing. He thoroughly enjoys introducing people to the wonders of the ocean.

Captain Tris Colket on his boat, *Last Mango*, at the canal behind his home on North Hutchinson Island in Fort Pierce.

Tris Colket in His Own Words

I was born in Pennsylvania in 1948 in Bryn Mawr Hospital in the suburbs of Philadelphia. We lived in a rural area and, like most fishermen, I think fishing is in our blood from the very start. I would spend days exploring the woods and the many streams and ponds and find trout, carp, crawdads, or tadpoles. We would catch carp on the proverbial "carp on dough ball" trick.

Streams were stocked with trout every spring, and that was the highlight of the year. We caught trout on worms. It was pretty basic, and we were in awe of the "professionals" who would show up with their little spinners and do much better than we did. We used bobbers, and

I had an old fishing pole with an Orvis fly reel on it given to me by my grandfather.

We moved to Florida in 1961, when I was thirteen. We lived on the river in Vero. My stepfather was an avid fisherman. His influence had a great deal to do with my fascination for fishing. He married my mother the year before we moved down here. They fished every year in the Marathon Bonefish Tournament in the Florida Keys and salmon fished in Nova Scotia.

My sister, Leslie, and I would go to the bonefish tournaments with them. They would rent a little skiff for us to use while they bone fished. The tournament was a huge event, and it was very exciting just to know that my parents were in it. It was a learning experience to be on our own in a boat, just my younger sister and me, and be responsible for it as well as our own survival.

We explored the flats and went under bridges where the tide was running at 6 knots. You know the way the Keys are. I was about fourteen, and Leslie was a few years younger. We tried to catch bonefish and never did, but it was just so exciting to see a lemon shark swimming by or to perhaps spy a bonefish or a permit. Barracuda were all over, and it was a thrill to see fish in the water. I'd like to think that flats fishing has maintained itself down there.

VERO BEACH

We caught snook in our backyard off the dock and off the seawall. That was fun. They went right from the river to the frying pan. It was magical and more tasty than the fish I had eaten when growing up in Pennsylvania.

FIRST BOAT

I think within a year or two we had a 16-foot boat with a 75-horsepower Johnson on the back of it. It wasn't too long before I was able go on my own in the river, even before I could drive. I didn't know any real good fishermen, but I did know how to catch snook and jack crevalle. I actually became a commercial fisherman in Vero at the early age of fourteen, catching jacks and selling them to Rice's Fish Camp for enough money to buy candy bars and Cokes.

It was a small-scale fish house, and there was also a crab factory up there in Vero, on the other side of the bridge. Rice's was on the north-east side of the old Merrill Barber Bridge, the old drawbridge, which was the only bridge in Vero at the time. It was tucked in there right near the city marina. The Stockwell Crab Factory was at the base of the south bridge in Vero where it joins the west side of the river. They processed blue crab there, and it was the most fabulous crabmeat and the only blue crab I ever ate that wasn't full of shells.

COLLEGE

I went through four years of college and graduated from Rollins College in 1970. I was a child of the '60s and can't remember much of it. I thought about going to law school, even took the LSATs and was accepted to Stetson Law School, but just couldn't do that. Can you imagine me a lawyer? Some of my friends were going out to live in communes and live alternative lifestyles, but fishing was waiting for me.

EARLY COMMERCIAL FISHING

It disappointed my mother when I went into commercial fishing. She expected me to become a professional of some sort. After paying for four years of college, that seems like a reasonable reaction. As you might guess, there's a story to explain my transition to commercial fishing.

My friend John, aka "Reverend Disco," Langfitt was one of my old fishing and water skiing buddies. John lived in Vero when I moved there and was a year ahead of me in school. Like me, he was a river rat. We ran together and fished and water skied a lot. He went off to school before me, and about the time I graduated, he returned to Vero.

John had a small Aqua Sport that had been set up for commercial kingfishing. It was an inboard with a little cabin, and he kept it at Charlie Lowe's Fish House on the west side of Fort Pierce's north bridge. One day he said, "You know, we can catch kingfish in this boat."

I had a little bit of an idea of how to do it, and although he had fished with our friend Jimmy Muller, he had yet to venture out on his own, so this was a big, new adventure for both of us. We trolled around for a little bit with our baits on the outriggers and saw everybody catching fish on the jerk bug. So we pulled a 150-foot bug line, without an electric reel, by hand and put the line down on the deck. It was piano wire and would tangle up in a heartbeat! We caught 200 pounds of kingfish and felt like we were true commercial fishermen. That's what hooked me on it, and I fished John's boat myself for a month or two with a fair amount of success.

When John came back one day and was a bit upset about mullet scales on the deck, he unwittingly launched my career in the commercial fishing world. A few weeks later I had my own kingfish boat, a 25-foot Jersey skiff that I bought from Billy Minuth. She was docked over by the Fort Pierce Coast Guard Station, and it was probably a good place for me, because I had hair down to my waist, and the guys at the fish house just didn't know quite what to think about me.

I was docked alongside of the "Yankee" Fort Pierce fishing crowd. Jake Jacobus, Frankie Breig, Billy Minuth, Tommy McHale, Jim Ryan, "Banana" Jack Albinson, Dick Smith, and Mike Weiner were a few of the interesting characters I recall. Most were from New York and New Jersey, and they all had slightly more tolerance for a long-haired hippie fisherman. There actually were days at the fish house when I didn't know whether I was going to live to unload my catch and escape or not with my life. It was a tough crowd of second- and third-generation fishermen.

Amazingly, the key to acceptance was at my fingertips. There's an old saying in the fishing world: "You are only as good as your last catch!" In my case this translated into earning the respect of my peers, and I did that in short order. I was "born to fish" and made my mark quickly! After a series of good catches, I was grudgingly accepted by all but a few of the old guard.

My new 25-foot lapstrake boat had a Chrysler 318, the most dependable gas engine ever made. Early on, it was a big challenge for me just to go out the inlet in the dark every morning. There weren't that many buoys in the inlet, and none of them were lighted at the time. The range markers were the key to a safe transit. I just fished one-day trips, and that was enough of a challenge for me for the longest time. I was fortunate to be there. Every day was an adventure. It was just glorious that I could follow my passion and make a living at it. And, of course, once that happens, it's a done deal.

Going out both Fort Pierce Inlet and Sebastian Inlet in the dark and not knowing what to expect were the initial challenges that I faced. I think I had a vague concept at first of the danger of an outgoing tide and an east wind at the inlets. It only took one really good adventure to figure that out. I did know enough not to try and turn around once I got into it. Even Fort Pierce on a hard ebb tide and a 15-knot easterly wind is messy. I didn't necessarily know to sneak around the end of either jetty, which was a great thing once you figure that out.

So I think my first trip in the dark out through the whole damn tide situation and waves to the sea buoy was a pretty harrowing adventure. All the boats were turning around and coming back in, so I had to go back through it again. Fort Pierce Inlet pales in comparison, of course, to Sebastian Inlet, but I was a more seasoned sailor or fisherman at that point. I held Sebastian in a place of great respect and took more care there.

I remember one morning when Short Day (Gene Hayes), who had the biggest boat in the fleet at that time, about a 45-footer, just about sank going out the Sebastian Inlet. It was the *Miss Bess*. Thank God I was on the radio. Back then, we all had CB radios and no LORANs [Long Range Navigation]. He had fallen off a wave and taken one through the windshield. Gene put it on the air, so he saved the day there for me. I turned around and skedaddled back to the fish house.

A lot of times, when you're coming back through the Sebastian Inlet, you had no choice. Even if it was nice going out, and you'd spend a day of fishing, you'd come back into a hard ebb tide and a 15-knot breeze. You want to get lined up sooner than you do in Fort Pierce. You can't just come around the corner and feel good about it.

There is Monster Hole on the south side. It's a big mistake to get caught there, because there's a big swell. Monster Hole is one of the notoriously great surfing spots in all of Florida, and, when conditions are right, there's a big swell and a big sandbar out there, which breaks way off shore of the inlet. It's right near the spot where you might want to sneak around. It's fine to go across on a flat, calm day—there's enough water there—but it's not a good place to get caught in a boat on a rough day. It could wipe out a big boat.

I have a story about coming in in the fog. The only place that I ever experienced fog, in all the years of commercial fishing in Florida and in the Carolinas, was Sebastian in the wintertime, which is when we fished there.

The fog came infrequently, but it happened a few times. The fog came in during the middle of the day. At Sebastian, it settled in a couple times after we got offshore. With no LORAN and only a CB radio, it's pretty damn tough to find that inlet. Oh, God, I found that inlet way too many times by pure luck and a little intuition.

Jerry Harrison was the only guy with a LORAN or radar; I can't remember which it was that he had. It only worked some of the time, so it wasn't a sure thing. But if you got a glimpse of what direction he was going in, that was always a clue. Or you have a rough idea just by the compass heading that you took out of the inlet in Sebastian. There's not a big drift there, because you never get that close to the Gulf Stream current, so you kind of fake it.

I came in one day when that fog was pea soup in the inlet, and I only figured out where I was when I realized that I was at Monster Hole [laughs] and started feeling these big swells lifting the boat up in the air. It was just pure luck, so I scooted back to the north a little bit, but it was a great indicator of where I was. Monster Hole's swells helped me find the Sebastian Inlet that day. I never saw the beach.

A narrow, shallow current runs through the Sebastian Inlet much faster than it does in Fort Pierce, so there are much more radical conditions on that ebb tide with an east wind. For the longest time, little boats or a couple of recreational anglers would sink there every year, and people would drown that close to shore just because they didn't know how to negotiate inlet conditions.

A DOUBLE WATERSPOUT

I remember a particular summer squall when I was kingfishing. It seemed like there were more waterspouts offshore for a few years in the '70s. You'd see them coming and kind of keep an eye on them, but it wasn't a major event where you ran for your life. Hell, if you were catching fish, you weren't going to go anywhere. So you'd watch them,

Double waterspouts near Daytona, much closer than the picture makes them appear.

and they'd pass offshore or go back up into the clouds. They had the potential to either drop down into the water or not.

One day I saw a double waterspout, both right next to each other, and they came towards me. I finally had to pick up and move. They seemed to want me badly. One day, I think it might have been the same day, I got out of their way, and I watched them go right up to Al Tyrrell's boat. He never moved. He just kept fishing. I remember hearing him on the radio saying it had damaged the boat's canopy, his shade top.

It's a wonder that I never experienced an actual lightning strike. I know a few fishermen who did. I think Al's boat attracted waterspouts and lightning a time or two. God knows why I've never been struck by lightning while swordfishing in the straits all summer. That lightning, those electrical storms and lightning bolts coming down everywhere, you feel that you're the highest point around as far as you can see, and the lightning's striking the water all around you.

WATERSPOUT

I had a waterspout take the canopy off the back of my kingfish boat. I was leaving West End, by myself, heading back to Fort Pierce. We'd been vacationing over there, and the rest of my family was flying back,

Thirty-four-foot *Isolde* in 1977, used for kingfishing and later for swordfishing.

because the kids were little at the time. I was on my 34-foot Webbers Cove single engine, the *Isolde.*

I'd left West End in risky weather conditions with a steady 15-to-20 breeze, not knowing there was a hurricane coming. Back then, you couldn't get a weather report. Sometimes, you still can't in the Bahamas without really good electronics. My VHF radio didn't pick up the weather over there, and the waterspout came within minutes of my leaving West End. The weather obscured my view of any land, and rain came down, and the seas were rough, and I was wishing I had never left. I turned around to go back, but there was no way I could. The shore had disappeared in the rainstorm. Back then, I didn't have a plotter or radar or anything. I doubt you could have shot the gap in the reef anyway. So I turned back around and decided, "I guess it's Fort Pierce."

I took a heading of 90 degrees, thinking the Gulf Stream would move me to the north (which it sometimes does), and the waterspout came down and ripped the flimsy green canopy off the boat. I never really saw it. It kind of came and went in a hurry, but it left its mark on the boat and on my . . . psyche and on my confidence in continuing the journey.

I got to Fort Pierce with a lot of luck. My LORAN went out in transit, and I finally saw the nuclear power plant. Found my way to the Fort Pierce Inlet and pulled in to the fish house, and somebody said, "What the hell are you doing?"

And I said, "I just came back from the Bahamas."

And they said, "Well, don't you know there's a hurricane coming?"

THE MAJOR STORM

The major storm event was years later, when I had the *Last Mango*, and I was shark fishing out of Fernandina Beach on the border of Florida and Georgia. Off of North Florida you can be forty-five or fifty miles offshore and still be in only 240 feet of water, which was about the deepest we could successfully set our gear. All you see out there are military naval ships; you don't even see freighters. I don't know where the heck they are, but they're not out there. We sometimes fished for days and never saw another boat. We were on the edge of the shelf, which is the last structure on the bottom before it starts meandering down into the deeper Gulf Stream waters.

There's some interesting live bottom there in 240 feet, because it's so far offshore, perhaps. Maybe it hasn't been dragged over by the rock-shrimp boats or the scallop boats as much, or maybe it's not fished as hard by recreational anglers, because it's so far offshore. The sharks migrate past there as part of their north-south migratory pattern.

We set twelve nautical miles of 900-pound test mono longline with 900 hooks. It doesn't quite meet up with the forty miles that you hear about on this new swordfish TV show, but it was a lot of gear.

I worked with two deckhands. Because it's close to the Gulf Stream, the current can pick up out there and run 3 knots. And that's what happened after we set our line this day. We set the gear in the evening and were going to pick it up the next morning. Overnight, the current picked up, and we could not get it off the bottom. It would just break from the stress of pulling it up in the current.

People may think you just sit there and wind in your line. You don't

Tris's boat, *Last Mango*, rigged for shark fishing. Today it is a classic charter boat.

do that. Even though it's being pulled up on a hydraulic spool, you have to be parallel to your gear and be in just the right spot so that there's a certain amount of ease to regain your line. You're never going to move that gear, first of all, because it's on the bottom and it's weighted down. Second, it's got fish on it, and third, it's often wrapped around stuff on the bottom. The boat has to be directly above it at all times or close to being on top of it, to pull it straight up so it doesn't hang up or break from the strain. In a strong current, it's essential that you are very close. You have to be spot on to get it back. But the combination of all those elements and 3 knots of current will still create enough strain that it'll break the 900-pound test line.

We couldn't get it back that day. We tried and broke it off a few times. We'd put a buoy every three-quarters of a mile, so there was a way to go to the next buoy and work your way back, if you could get [the line] up at the next buoy. We played around with it for most of the day and didn't really get much of it up. We were 100 miles from the dock in Daytona. Ordinarily, we'd just go inshore and anchor up and hope that the tide eased up over the next night. That was our plan.

The forecast was 15 to 20 the next day, which isn't exactly ideal, but because of all our gear (it's a huge investment), we were going to stay. We came back into 160 feet and anchored. It was starting to get dark, and a swordfish boat came by on his way into the inlet at Fernandina. He gave me a shout on the radio just to see if everything was all right.

And I said, "Yeah, it's fine. We don't like the forecast much, but we need to pick our gear back up, so we're sticking it out."

He said, "Did you listen to the forecast?"

And I said, "Yeah, it's 15 to 20, out of the southeast," thinking he's a swordfish boat and that's going to seem reasonable to him.

He said, "Do you happen to have a sideband? Did you happen to listen to the sideband forecast?"

And I said, "No, I don't have a sideband radio."

He said, "They're calling for gale-force winds on the sideband."

Well, we were anchored. It was sloppy as hell already. It would have been a big pain to get the anchor up. Although we could have done that, it would have been a dangerous trip in high seas to an unfamiliar inlet. We would have arrived at Fernandina in the dark. It wasn't an inlet that I wanted to go through at night in six- to eight-foot seas. I guess that's why we stuck it out. We were 100 miles from Daytona, and we had been warned. But you know, the one thing about commercial fishing that's so great, and it makes me proud to be a part of it, is that the responsibility you take for what you're doing, how you're doing it, and who you're fishing with (if you have deckhands) is purely yours. No excuses are going to make a difference. And I think that's such an important part of commercial fishing and our lifestyle. I made one of those tough decisions, which was to stay. It may have been one of my less well thought out decisions, but we stuck it out on the ocean.

The sea conditions turned into a nightmare. It was unlike anything I'd experienced in thirty-five years of fishing. We did have an eight-man automatic life raft in a fiberglass container on the top of the pilot house, but it was so rough that I'm absolutely sure we wouldn't have been able to launch it successfully. You couldn't stand up to move. The boat was lurching and jumping so, you had to crawl. I would guess that the seas were twelve to fourteen feet. We were anchored in a 40-foot boat, and we all had kind of a wide-eyed, deer-in-the-headlights look. My crew's trusting me, and I'm thinking, "Well, at this point it's time for a prayer, because there's nothing you can really do when things get that bad." That's when bad things happen in the ocean, when sea conditions are so radical that normal preventive measures that you might take are impossible. Something like fixing a bilge pump or whatever was almost impossible in those conditions (which, fortunately, I didn't have to do).

I'm convinced the wind was blowing so hard, I'd say at least 60 knots plus, that it would have ripped the life raft all to pieces if we deployed it, or it would have blown away before we had ever gotten in it [laughs]. If you'd pulled that string and inflated it, it would have been gone so fast, you would have wondered what happened. So that's how scary it was.

I had an Italian journalist on board who was doing a story for an Italian travel magazine called *Gulliver*. His assignment was an article on shark fishing around the world. So in the previous and much calmer two days, he had been in the water taking pictures of sharks as they were coming up on the line. We'd had two really nice days and had put lots of fish on the boat, and then this. The shark line was still out, and we were hoping to pick it up that next day and head home. Sergio, the Italian journalist, was on board. He was a professional and an adventurous journalist who got into the water to film the sharks and was doing it right, but this was a bad choice of trips because of the storm.

Conditions got worse, and, at one point, I saw a ship and wanted to let him know we were there. As I mentioned earlier, the only boats we ever saw out there were naval ships. We were too far offshore to call the Coast Guard. VHF only travels so far, and in these conditions it was impossible. So we were on our own. I raised the ship on Channel 16, which was a bit of a surprise. The boat was lurching, and it was just by chance that he came back. I thought, "Oh, here's a little security."

He said, "Do you need assistance?"

This was still relatively early in the night. I said, "I'm not sure what you could do. I feel like we're in a really bad spot here."

And he said, "Do you need assistance?"

And I said, "What kind of assistance could you offer?"

He said, "I don't know. That would be up to you, Captain." That wasn't really a good answer. It was too rough to abandon ship, and I wasn't going to do that anyway!

So I said, "The best thing that I could hear from you would be that you would stand by in the area to render assistance if necessary."

He said that he saw our light but was having trouble hearing us. I wondered if the antenna had been torn off, but, amazingly, it stayed, and I thought I would have somebody to call if things deteriorated past that point.

He said, "We'll be standing by."

By the time things got really scary [laughs], I couldn't raise them on the radio anymore, so that was a one-time shot, and the conditions got worse.

This was probably nine o'clock at night. By ten thirty, the waves were coming over the bow, slamming into the windshield, going over the whole boat and actually coming back into the boat on the sides a little bit. But the boat was dealing with it well enough. It was frightening. At about eleven o'clock in the evening the conditions were impossible. And then they got worse. We were unable to move around in the boat other than to crawl, and that was dangerous, too. We needed to just stay put, jammed up somewhere. We had two bilge pumps pumping out any water that got below decks. We went down in the cabin. It seems like that would be a horrible place to be [laughs] in that storm, but we were so tired that we just wanted to lie down in the bunks.

Sergio, the journalist, had his sleeping bag out across the deck and tucked in by the main bulkhead at the helm when a wave came completely over the boat and broke two of the pilothouse windows. We heard this horrible crash, and it sounded like a combination of this giant wave crushing the front of the boat and the windows breaking. Amazingly, it didn't really crush anything, but it came through the windshield and broke two of the four glass panes. They were made of that laminated glass that had the film in the middle of it so that it didn't shatter and was held in place by the rubber gaskets on the sides. Each piece of glass weighed about fifteen pounds and was about three feet by three feet. One of them cracked in a bunch of pieces, and one just got bent in half and came down on Sergio's head.

Well, just the noise of all that happening and hearing the water coming into the boat through the windows was really terrifying. We had the deck lights on and lights on in the cabin. The next thing I saw was Sergio's face looking in at us, and it was bright red. The window cut his head in an eight-inch gash all the way to the skull, and you know how head wounds bleed. We had the shit scared out of us, and then Sergio looks in from the deck with his face covered with blood, and I thought I'd died and gone to hell.

There wasn't anything to do. We could barely move. We took care of Sergio as best we could. Then he went into shock. We wrapped him in a blanket, held some clean T-shirts on his head to stop the bleeding, and we put him down in the cabin. By then he was immobile and wasn't doing anything. We may not have followed the guidelines for shock to the nth degree, but we made him comfortable and kept him warm and got him out of the weather.

At this point in time, the waves were not only breaking over the bow of the boat, but they were coming in the boat because the windows were gone, and we couldn't do much about it. We managed to get Sergio below deck. The *Mango* was built well, with Freeman hatches in the deck and big scuppers in the transom. The waves and water just went right through. It wasn't great, but it was okay.

The aspect of this particular event that made it so profound was that there was nothing we could do. We had life jackets nearby. Oddly enough, we didn't put them on. In retrospect, I wonder why we didn't. Maybe it was the power of positive thought that we still felt we'd make it through. Or maybe I didn't want to alarm the crew. However, I did think about that life raft all through the night and that it's not going to help us because of how strong the wind was blowing. But we survived the night.

MORNING AFTER

By morning, it had subsided. We'd actually gotten some sleep. By then, it was probably eight- to ten-foot seas with a light breeze. During the storm, I had cranked up the diesel engine in case the anchor line broke, because you can only imagine trying to keep the boat into the seas or to keep from capsizing without steerage. If the anchor line broke it would have been a very dangerous situation. I think I had started the diesel even prior to the wave crashing through and breaking the windows.

However, in the morning we realized we would be able to limp to shore and were plenty ready to leave that whole longline where it was. I was worried about Sergio, because he had a head wound. There's a time frame there for stitches, and I was concerned about him. We were still too far offshore to call the Coast Guard, and the boat was running. Sergio was very sedate. He was conscious, but he wasn't talking. Not from lack of blood or anything like that—that wasn't a concern, and that had stopped relatively quickly—but his red face served its purpose by scaring the shit out of all of us.

So we got ready to haul the anchor up, and when I put it into gear, it stopped. The propeller stopped turning. Well, during the night the tag end of the anchor line had washed over the bow, and in the course of the engine running all night long with that little bit of drag that's on the transmission and the propeller shaft slowly turning and everything, the prop had wound the tail end of the anchor line all around the propeller. Had the anchor line broken, with no power or steerage, we would have capsized for sure.

So here we were. We have survived this storm from hell, but we can't head for home because our five-eighths-inch anchor line's wrapped up in the propeller.

Well, you know what you do? You go overboard and cut it out . . . in eight-foot seas. Going under the boat in eight-foot seas while it's going up and down was about the most dangerous thing next to being out there in that storm to start with. So, as the captain and the only willing volunteer, I went overboard. I thought about tying a rope on, so if I got knocked out, at least my deck hands would be able to pull me out from under the boat, but I didn't, and in hindsight, it was not smart. It made it a little bit more dangerous. But we did have a line trailing out the back.

I went down there and cut that five-eighths-inch line out from under the boat in eight-foot seas for about an hour. I had no dive tank. I was in pretty good shape, and I had been holding my breath all night [laughs].

About the first time that the prop went up and came down right by my face, I realized how big a deal it was. These seas were every bit of eight feet. You're holding onto the shaft, and you hope that there's not a whole lot of distance between your head and the hull, because you're kind of riding on the bottom of the boat and avoiding the prop. I had shut the engine down. I never would go under the boat with the engine running, just in case somebody hit that shift lever by mistake or something.

After more than an hour to get the line out, we opted to head for home. We were 40 miles from Fernandina and about 90 to 100 miles from our home port in Daytona. We headed for home.

AT THE DOCK

We got back to the dock around midnight that next night, because the boat was a 9-knot boat at that point in time. I think we got Sergio to drink some water, and I can't remember much else. We were all so glad to be alive. We just slept on the ride home and got over the scare. We worried about Sergio, but there wasn't much we could do about that either.

We got back to the dock, and it was supposed to be such a big deal that Sergio had hired a photographer who worked for *National Geographic* to meet us and come along. The guy smoked clove cigarettes, and he was a character. He lived in Aspen, Colorado. The reason I know this is we got back to the dock at midnight, and here's this guy, sitting on the dock, smoking clove cigarettes, seemed just wacko as hell. I don't know why; that's just who he was.

And Sergio recognized him, and the first words out of Sergio's mouth since the storm began was, "Dhesa guys! Dhey trya to keela me!" [laughs]. I swear. He hasn't said a word in twenty-four hours, and he says, "Dhesa guys! Dhey trya to keela me!"

The National Marine Fisheries Service had put him in touch with me because I had tagged a lot of sharks throughout my shark-fishing career. I was good friends with this guy, Jack Casey, up in Narragansett, Rhode Island. They have a lab up there, and he is the father of their shark-tagging program. Very interesting guy. He and his staff were all National Marine Fisheries Service employees. I worked closely with them with their tagging effort. So, since Jack was kind of the father of the shark world up there, this journalist had put out feelers and was put in touch with Jack. Jack put him in touch with me, and the rest is history. And Sergio went on our most infamous shark-fishing trip.

A GLORIOUS TIME

I kingfished at just the right time. It was still in its heyday. It was such a glorious part of Fort Pierce's history and a great time for me, fishing with all the second- and third-generation fishermen who were involved in kingfishing, net fishing, and river fishing. I wish I had been able to document it better, because it was something wonderful that will be lost forever.

What nearly ruined kingfishing, as I see it, goes back to the net fishing. The roller-rig net fishing that transitioned from bluefish and Spanish mackerel to kingfish in the late '70s marked the death knell to what was an industry that I thought would last forever. The king mackerel fishery has actually come back since we got rid of the net boats. Hook-and-line kingfishing is far less intrusive than net fishing. You give a fish a choice of biting a lure or bait, or not. Kingfish would shut down and stop biting, for whatever reason, when you're hook-and-line fishing. They can't shut down or avoid being caught in a net. Nets were a very efficient way to wipe out the kingfish population. And with the airplanes spotting the fish for the nets, they were incredibly effective.

One of the interesting things that happened out there off of Fort Pierce, quite often, was when the spotter planes came out, they would find the biggest schools of kingfish right under a kingfish boat, because we would have figured out how to find the fish by less sophisticated measures. I actually had net boats come out and set a circle of net around my boat via the spotter plane, which would radio them and tell them exactly when to turn, how tight to make their circle, and how to wrap up that school of fish. Once they did that, the fish stopped biting, and we went back to the dock. They not only stopped biting that day, but once the nets were set, they pretty much stopped biting, period.

As hand-line kingfishermen, we felt a combination of anger and frustration, and there really was not anything we could do. The fact that we were losing our ability to make a living seemed to be such an unfair and unnecessary and unattractive way. It was just disastrous, and sad.[1]

SWORDFISHING

In the mid-'70s, when kingfishing was still a viable option, we swordfished in the summer and kingfished in the winter in the Florida Straits for about three years. I had a 34-foot fiberglass boat at that time, the *Isolde*, which was relatively small for swordfishing. Everett Harrison and I got together and decided we were going to swordfish my boat. There'd been one summer before that that I saw some of the local boats,

---

1 Over the years, kingfishing has rebounded to some degree, but not before many hook-and-liners lost their livelihood and abandoned fishing to find jobs elsewhere.

Tris and a healthy catch of swordfish.

31-foot Stapletons and other boats, go out swordfishing just for one-day trips. And they did well.

So Everett and I built a longline spool out of a stainless steel propeller shaft, and we cut three-foot circles out of three-quarter-inch plywood laminated together and secured the plywood sides with stainless backing plates welded to the stainless shaft. We had a 12-volt electric bomb bay door motor power the reel, and it worked fine setting the gear out [laughs]. But when the gear started coming in on our very first set, the pressure of the line winding up on the spool just spread out the plywood sides till they rubbed on the frame, and the motor couldn't turn it. We had to turn it by hand. Fortunately, we only had six miles of line to get in, and we had a great catch.

For me swordfishing lasted only a few years in the mid-'70s in the middle of my kingfishing days. It happened all of a sudden, almost overnight. One summer no one was swordfishing; the next summer, guys were coming in with huge catches. No one had known there were swordfish here. This was when anyone could go out and catch them. I fished a 34-foot boat and had anywhere from six to eight miles of line. It was like a gold rush.

We couldn't even get the gear. There was such a run on swordfishing gear down here, we didn't have the right contacts and didn't know

A triple marker swordfish.

how to buy the tarred line and stainless clips. When I first started swordfishing, we ended up with black eighth-inch tarred line. When we couldn't get that, we got big shanks of yellow ski rope. The damn stuff floated, so we had to put lead inserts in every seventy feet or so. There were a lot of them [leads], and they would work themselves halfway out and cause problems. The black line sank by itself. We put out six miles of line and floated it with crab-trap buoys.

It's amazing that we did so well. We were really behind the curve with most of our gear, and that's a bad thing in the commercial fishing world. It turns out, once the crab-trap buoys pulled under water by the big swords we were catching, they get crushed and don't have any flotation, so that was a bad idea. The bullet buoys that they use now retain a certain amount of their flotation even when they're pulled down.

Anyway, we put the line out first time we'd ever been swordfishing on my boat, and we caught fifteen hundred pounds of markers.[2] We never caught a fish under 200 pounds the first few trips we made. They were all big, 200- to 400-pound dressed fish. But that 12-volt

---

2 Swordfish are graded by headed and gutted carcass size as follows: 34–49 pounds, 50–99 pounds, and over 100 pounds. The last are called "markers." A 200-pound carcass is called a "double marker," a 300-pound, a "triple marker."

motor wouldn't haul the line in, so we ended up having to spin the rim of the spool by hand to bring back all that line.

Somehow we made an improvement on the electric motor. Back then, I never had hydraulics. Hell, there were guys fishing two miles of line and pulling it all in by hand. That was the old days.

Swordfishing was going on up north, but I don't think anyone knew that the swordfish were here in the Straits. There was swordfishing going on in New England, for sure. That goes back to the '50s, I believe. I suppose it had not occurred to them that the swordfish would live in the warmer waters down here. As it turns out, they migrate all the way through here and down past Puerto Rico. Markers are over 100 pounds. There is a marker, a double marker, and a triple marker. It's all by hundreds.

In rapid succession, year to year, the size of the fish diminished drastically. After three years of fishing my small boat, it was apparent to me that the only way to be successful in the swordfishing world would be to travel. By then, there were big boats down here, mostly 50- to 60-foot boats fishing out of Florida ports. They were going to Puerto Rico in the winter, and they were fishing relatively small boats in New England.

There were a couple of guys who stuck it out, like Gary Warner and a couple of others. I have to wonder how successful they were. There was not a big enough population of swordfish for all those boats to do well here. The catches got smaller and smaller, so that's when I started traveling more in the kingfishing world. I traveled for kingfish up to Daytona with Al Tyrrell, Lewis Wells, Frankie Breig, and Clyde Marshall. Our first summer swordfishing, we averaged well over twelve hundred pounds a set. It was great. The mid-'70s were the heyday of swordfishing in the Florida Straits.

PONCE INLET RESCUE

Al [Tyrrell], Lewis Wells, and I and a couple other kingfish guys had gone up to Ponce Inlet. Lewis Wells and I ended up staying up there and shark fishing for one year after the kingfishing had migrated north. Shark fishing became something to fill in the gaps in the fishing year and evolved from there.

Ponce Inlet was always evolving. Shifting currents continually built up sandbars in Ponce, and large dredges were often working for months to keep the channel navigable. It was always kind of a challenge, because we'd go out fishing, and five days later we'd come back, and the dredge had moved to the other side of the inlet, and the pipes were going in a different direction. Navigating the dredge pipes when they were dredging the inlet was always a challenge.

We came in one day and on our approach noticed a 40-foot Coast Guard boat operating in the inlet and then outside the inlet. As we turned the corner of the north jetty, we saw a capsized outboard boat in the inlet. We couldn't understand why the Coast Guard was not going over to help these people. There were two women and a guy in the water and they were hanging onto their boat, which was overturned and drifting close to breaking waves, just offshore of the south jetty. The Coast Guard was motoring around and about. We thought they must have the situation under control. But it became apparent when they settled in a spot outside the inlet that they were waiting for the overturned boat to drift out the inlet and through some very nasty breaking waves at the end of the south jetty before their rescue effort could begin. I guess it was too shallow to get their larger boat up there near the breakers.

It seemed obvious to me that we should go get those people out of harm's way. We motored over there, and I spun the boat around and backed up to them, and it was a little bit scary. It would have been trouble if we drifted any further out the inlet. This was a shark-fishing trip, and I had two deckhands on board who helped. The people in the water didn't want to let go of the boat and swim to us, even though we were only ten feet away. I really couldn't go any closer to them. We persuaded the two girls to swim to the boat. We have a door in the back of the boat for bringing in big sharks and swordfish. We pulled the two girls right through the door with no problem at all.

Here we are drifting closer and closer to disaster, and the guy won't let go of his boat. His boat is upside down, and he wants me to tow it in. You know, it's his baby. I finally had to say, "Listen, buddy, it's either your boat or my boat, but you can't have it both ways." It was a dicey situation. By the time he let go of his boat and swam to my boat, I was within seconds of just saying, "I'm sorry. I've got to go." But I'm thinking that's not good, because I've offered to help this guy, and now I'm going to leave him. He finally swam for it, and we hauled him through the tuna door and in the boat.

We motored back to the deep water on the north side of the inlet, and lo and behold, who's there but the Coast Guard, suggesting that we immediately transfer these people onto their boat in some very rough water. No one would pull their nice boat up to a big ol' metal Coast Guard boat in a rough inlet. So I had to tell the Coast Guard, "No way. Why don't we motor into the river, and I'll offload them there?"

We did. And these young people all said, "Thank you very much." We had wrapped them up in towels and blankets; they were already kind of cold and . . . that was it. Never heard a word from you know who. No "Thank-yous" from the Coast Guard. That's my rescue story.

FRANKIE AND TERRY BREIG

Frankie Breig was the original traveler in the world of kingfishing. He and his wife, Terry Breig, were fishing together when I started kingfishing in 1970, and Pappy [Terrel] Hayes was also fishing the *Aurora*, a big old wooden boat. Terry and Frankie fished together a long time. She was as good a "fisherman" as any guy. I was a rookie on the block when I started kingfishing, so I wasn't hanging out with Frankie at the time, but I used to see them in Sebastian, and at Charlie Lowe's fish house in Fort Pierce, unloading more kingfish than I could imagine. They were good; they were great. Steve Lowe, Tommy McHale, Ish Taylor, Flash, and a few other guys who always managed to catch more fish than everybody else—Frankie was definitely one of those guys.

U-HAULING FISH

In the 1970s and early 1980s very few of us traveled. For most kingfishermen a big trip was from Fort Pierce to Sebastian or Jupiter, and only some of us went to either place. Sebastian Inlet's not necessarily the greatest place to fish out of in the winter. And when the kingfish were coming down, we'd go there, because the fishing was that much better. Eventually, we'd end up back in Fort Pierce. Going up to the New Smyrna/Daytona area was a big deal back then.

Lewis Wells, Al Tyrrell, and myself started out fishing for Paul Pickett up there at Sea Harvest in New Smyrna and then moved up to the north side of the inlet, to Inlet Harbor, which was a cool old place with old-timey fishing docks but not necessarily a fish house. We would get together and ship our fish back to Fort Pierce. It was brutal.

We had big fish boxes at the dock, and sometimes we'd keep our catch for two days. We used plenty of ice. We loaded fish to the U-Haul with a garbage can full of fish, pull them out, being careful not to stab each other with the spines, throw them in the U-Haul, ice them down, tarp them down. We put tarps between each person's fish. My pickup truck held three thousand pounds of kingfish, plus the U-Haul trailer. So we'd split it up and find a way to separate the fish for the three of us and haul it down to Triple-M Seafood in Fort Pierce, where we got twice as much for our fish.

When we found that out, we were kicking ourselves for not having found it out sooner. We were selling our fish so cheap up there and had just assumed that there was no alternative, and in a way, there really was not. The fishing was so good up there that you could sell your fish for less and still come out better than you would down here. Before we had quotas and trip limits on our catches, we'd fish from daylight till dark. That was the deal. It was a long day. It was not unusual to catch a thousand to fifteen hundred pounds a day.

Let me give you a Lewis Wells–Al Tyrrell story. Al Tyrrell has always had a yellow station wagon with wood panels on the side. It's not the same one, but he has one today, forty years later. I was driving my truck with a ton of kingfish iced in the bed and a trailerful behind. He and Lewis were following me down I-95 to Fort Pierce to sell them at Triple-M Seafood. I saw them creeping up behind me, and they were laughing and giggling as they pulled alongside. I didn't have anybody to talk to, so when they faded back a bit, I took my white boots off and put them on my hands while I was driving down the highway at 75 miles per hour. It made it look like I was driving the truck with my feet.

The next time they came by, they saw me driving all their fish to Fort Pierce with my feet [laughs]. I knew from their reaction that they were wondering if their hard-earned catches would survive the trip.

We had to switch U-Haul rental agents a time or two. Those trailers were never the same after the trips from Daytona to Fort Pierce loaded with kingfish.

BIGGEST KINGFISH CATCH

One day I hit the 2,000-plus mark fishing by myself. The fishing out of Ponce Inlet was so good that I wanted to get back offshore quickly, so I took my big catch to a fish house down in Oak Hill. This place catered mostly to the net-fishing crowd there on Mosquito Lagoon. Because of the notoriously low prices in north Florida as a whole, we agreed that they were going give me a minimum price. There was evidently some misunderstanding regarding the word "minimum"! My biggest catch brought the worst price I ever got for kings. So much for hitting the 2,000-pound mark!

KINGFISHING GEAR

I got in at the tail end of that spoonfishing that you hear about. It must have been great. There was a time when people used lead cannonballs instead of paravanes.[3] Billy Minuth would talk about five-foot cables with thirty feet of mono to a spoon. Catching fish that close to the boat took less time and resulted in a big catch, for sure. Every time I tried stuff like that, the fish shut off, they stopped biting. I never saw a time when the kings were that hungry. I'm sure that happened.

Even today, Al goes out and catches fish on spoons when everybody else is fishing bait. But you definitely have to find your own fish, and you have to find them at just the right time. I think there were a lot of fish caught on the bug. The bug line was probably shorter. You could catch kingfish well on 135 to 150 feet of wire back then. Tommy McHale was the best jerk-bug fisherman. Oh, man, he was something. He cut that circle so tight. I could never figure out how he made that work.

SHARK FISHING

I have George Kaul to thank for my success in the shark-fishing world. George had a one-mile spool, almost a toy, but it was hydraulic and very rugged. I heard him one day on the radio (imagine that) say that he wanted to get rid of it. I had a kind of a curiosity about what I might be able to catch with this short piece of gear.

My first shark-fishing effort was just an experiment, and we set it out and floated it, offshore of the bar. We probably were only using fifty

---

3 A paravane is more commonly known as a planer.

Packed and dressed out sharks on the *Last Mango*.

hooks back then. We were just trying it out here in Fort Pierce. I used old swordfish stuff for it. I still had big ol' J hooks left over from the first effort in swordfishing, before we refined our tackle.

Year by year, we refined a lot of tackle to keep up with what was going on. And we caught sharks on the surface, and nobody wanted to buy them, initially. But then Triple-M would buy them. Then you'd wait to see whether they could sell them or not and whether they would pay you for shark. It was pretty iffy.

You have to dress sharks out differently. You can't leave the belly flaps on shark. Sharks excrete urine through their skin. And, primarily, they excrete through the skin in their belly. So the combination of the fact that that was the area in the shark that had the concentration of, it's called uric acid, and that the dressed-out shark was a nicer commodity with some of that belly flap cut off—the combination of those two elements, I think, led to what the buyers expected, which was a shark that had the belly cut off, kind of even with the rest of the body and then the head's cut off, and the neck's dressed back so the gills are out and cut off, too. It's just a torpedo of shark meat. And that's a trick in itself with the skin and dressing it out just so.

We caught ten or fifteen out here when we first started playing around with it. We caught a lot of big tiger sharks off Fort Pierce. These would be thousand pounders, no doubt about it. They looked like little submarines when they come up behind the boat. It was a little bit scary.

I had quite an arsenal by the time I was finished shark fishing. I tried every kind of gun I could get my hands on. Most effective, without a doubt, hands down, was a 12-gauge shotgun with birdshot. Sharks have such a primitive neurological system and a very small brain, so it was difficult to really pinpoint that spot. And even if you put a slug through it, it didn't necessarily slow him as much as a very tight pattern of birdshot, and the birdshot was cheaper. You put the barrel of the shotgun very close to the fish, so it doesn't spread out very far. You don't jam it right up to it. But, it turned out, eventually, we had to get away from that because the pellets would migrate. They would go into the shark, and then they'd migrate up into the meat on occasion. And that wasn't a great way to sell any kind of fish—with birdshot in it. We switched to different things. We ended up finding that a .357 with just a light load in it was as good as anything.

Thousand-pound tigers and thousand-pound hammerheads were the biggest sharks that we caught. And that was a fairly frequent circumstance. The majority of the sharks, of course, were much smaller, and the shark that we were looking for and targeting was something called a sandbar shark. They are commonly known as the sand shark. They're not the same as a nurse shark.

Very few people really know which shark is which. And that was one of the fun things about shark fishing for me: discovering. Nobody knew. And that's how I met this guy, Jose Castro [Ray Perez also collaborated and became friends with Jose Castro], who was one of the leading experts in the world of sharks. He had written a book that was my bible in terms of which sharks were which. At the time, I knew more about what I was selling to markets than the marketplace knew what they were buying, and it took them awhile to figure it out. I suggested a shark guide written by Jose Castro. It had really good descriptions, pictures, and identifications.

There's a very slight difference between many, many species of sharks that the average person wouldn't possibly know or distinguish by looking at them, even side by side. So the shark dealers and buyers were at a loss. I had this natural curiosity and was seeing the sharks as a whole fish, as opposed to what went to market. It made it even more difficult for anyone seeing the shark once it was cut up.

It didn't take me long to figure out that hammerheads and tiger sharks were not desirable for the marketplace. The blacktip shark is an especially nice shark, and if I were going to eat a shark, I would choose a blacktip. Spinners, which people mistake for blacktips, are so similar that you might not ever tell the difference, are also good. They get bigger.

There actually is no sand shark. The sand shark was a catchall over time for any shark that looked kind of like your average shark. But there's something called a sandbar shark, also called a brown shark, which is what we targeted. That was the most profitable and easy to find in large schools. Now they're off the list; you're not allowed to catch them. They've been overfished. Bull sharks were relatively common to catch, but not in large numbers. The biggest schools of sharks were always blacktips, spinners, or sandbars. So if you could figure out where they were, it'd be like finding a big school of kingfish.

We had a hydraulic spool that was very powerful that brought the line into the boat. We pulled the fish in through the door in the transom by hand. And a 1,000-pound fish was a test. Sometimes we would take the main line spool and get it out over the tail of the shark and have it going up to the davit, then try to lift up the tail so that it would help us slide it in headfirst.

I had a canopy over the whole boat to get out of the sun. You don't want to spend your life standing in the sun if you could help it, so we were working under cover, and there was no way to lift or raise a big shark up on a huge davit over top of us to the deck, because the canopy was there.

SHARK BITE

Most of the time they were still alive, and even shooting them, because of their primitive nervous system, did not keep them from trying to bite you. Several times I had to cut one of my deckhands' feet out the mouth of a shark, where he just stepped down in the wrong place, and the shark chomped down on his boot.

The sharks are probably a little less aggressive once they're in the boat and having been shot through the head than they are in the wild. They don't have the ability to kind of thrash around as much. A lot of times it was more of a primitive reaction that made them chomp down. There's no mistaking the fact that once they bit down, you couldn't open their mouth back up, even when they were half dead. The only way I found to get them back open was to get a knife in between the boot and the inside of the teeth and cut the jaw so it opened up on one side. I did that a couple of times.

The crew members mostly stayed on, and more often than not, that bite was just a lot of pressure. You wouldn't have wanted to be barefoot and have that happen. But with a big boot on, you had a bit of a cushion. When you think about that, you picture some huge shark jaw but, most of the time, these were probably smaller six-foot sharks that we were catching, so their teeth weren't huge. They couldn't bite your toe or foot off.

SAND TIGER

The sand tiger is an interesting shark. This is what I caught for Sea World, because they're the only sharks that really swim with their teeth

Sand tiger shark extending its jaws as it would for feeding. What appears here to be a mounted fish is actually a live shark whose picture was taken on the deck of the *Last Mango*. Most of the sand tigers caught on the *Mango* where kept alive and trucked to Sea World.

exposed. When you go to Sea World and you see those sharks swimming with their teeth out, they're sand tigers. These were particularly vicious. I had one that we put in the fish box. They're like nurse sharks and can pump water through their gills. They're one of the only sharks that can stay still and survive. We'd put a wash-down hose in the fish box, and I had a big, heavy wash down with a two-inch pump. We kept him alive by cycling fresh saltwater in there. They're very complacent underwater in a tank in the fish box. They'd curl around a little bit because they were too long to fit in there. It wasn't terribly comfortable. Like a nurse shark, they'd just sit on the bottom.

We'd get back to the dock and wait forever for Sea World to come, because they were never on time. I was doing something over top of one of the tanks, and I had the cover off, when one came up out of the water. It just missed my arm. This is a 150-pound shark, okay? If that grabs your arm, it'd pull you into the tank. I don't know whether you'd bleed to death or drown before somebody got you out of there, but it wouldn't have been a good experience.

GREAT WHITE SHARKS

The great white was a mystery fish and an oddity in Florida waters. I'd never seen one before. We were fishing at that time twelve miles of line and a thousand hooks. So we covered some ground. It was always great when it came back filled up with fish and was always a real bummer when it didn't have anything on it. Water temperatures, water color, and the basic migratory habits were all important. You just really didn't want to set it in the wrong place. It took three hours to set a thousand-hook line.

The first white actually came up eight miles east of Daytona Beach in shallow water. These were juvenile great whites. The biggest one I caught was only 800 plus, and that's small for a great white. I caught three in a two-year period, and there were plenty more caught once the people knew what they were. I have a feeling there had been great whites caught in the past and not identified. I had to insist that that was a great white when I took it back, because all the fishermen said no. No one believed me that it was a great white.

I had Grant Gilmore come up from Harbor Branch because he was very interested in doing a dissection of it. So we kept it for him. He iden-

Great White Shark
Female est. 2-3yrs.
Daytona Beach
450 lbs.
3/25/85
9'3"

Tris and a nine-foot-three-inch, 450-pound great white shark caught off of Daytona Beach in 1985. The boat is the *Isolde*.

tified it as an immature female. We estimated the weight at 800 plus, and then I saved it in the cooler of the local restaurant at Inlet Harbor, because George Burgess, the shark expert from the University of Florida, got the shark, and Grant got the reproductive system and the insides.

I knew it was a great white because of my curiosity regarding the different species. I was familiar with everything that we caught, and this was not anything that we had caught before. It fit the description of a great white.

Lizzy (*left*), Tristram (*right*), and father, Captain Tris, with great white jaws.

It was legal to catch them then. It's not now; they're protected. A lot of sharks are protected now, which is a good thing. I fought that battle in my mind and with the National Marine Fisheries Service for years. But it's a resource, and there's no doubt in my mind that with many things, including most fish, that they're overtaxed as a resource. There are too many people and not enough fish.

We all thought, back in the '60s, maybe into the '70s, that there was an unlimited supply of natural resources. It's taken our culture and other cultures around the world lots of time to actually realize just how sacred and how special resources are, and how delicate they are. I don't have any problem saying that.

BIGGEST SHARKS

I have a picture of my son with the tail of a hammerhead that was thirteen feet long. I heard a story about a thirteen-foot hammerhead just the other day. I caught lots of sharks, and most of them were smaller. A 1,000-pound shark is a mighty big shark. You don't see a creature like

Crewmates Mike Flanagan and Mike Swanson hold up a large hammerhead shark caught east of Daytona Beach in about 120 feet of water.

that often. As many sharks as I caught, there were bound to be some big ones, and there were.

SHARK MARKET

It took some time, but the market eventually figured out that some shark species were better than others. Most of the sharks I was catching and selling were going to eventually find their way into Kroger and Winn-Dixie, right into the supermarket chains. Not from me

Thirteen-foot, thousand-pound tiger shark caught northeast of Fort Pierce, Florida. Deckhands Mike Flanagan and Mike Swanson prepare to dress the fish out for market.

directly, of course; there's all the middlemen who are part of that process.

We tagged some big sharks. But an awful lot of the sharks I tagged were tiger sharks. One of the places that I fished must have been a puppying ground or a nursery ground. These were sharks that were less than a year old. Occasionally we caught a lot of baby tiger sharks. Tiger sharks actually were not a species of interest for the market, so

This large great white shark was one of Tris's earliest catches. Here Tris's son, Tristram, looks into its jaws on the Triple M Seafood's fish house dock in Fort Pierce. The shark's body was sold for food.

we let them all go. Initially, we were keeping the big ones and selling them, but that changed after a while. These were smaller sharks which weren't of interest to us and had little value.

CONSERVATION

I always liked the idea of giving something back, because, as a fisherman, I feel fortunate to be able to reap the benefits of the natural resources. I always felt that it was rewarding to me if there was anything that I could do to help the fishery. Commercial fishing is almost a selfish thing, in a way. Not totally altruistic but nice that there were things that I could do that made me feel that I wasn't just taking from the resource and not making an effort to do something to give back to it.

So I enjoyed the combination of tagging sharks and saving specimens for a couple of different scientists. I also tagged sharks for Grant Gilmore and Jose Castro, who are both well known in the shark world as experts in their field. We even took scientists from the NMFS Narragansett Lab on occasional trips, scientists who do their own tagging and take their own measurements and get a feel for what it was like being out on a shark-fishing trip.

I tagged over 2,500 sharks during the time that I shark fished. It was great until their program ran out of money. When their funding stopped or slowed, their ability to correlate or disperse the information became problematic. For the longest time, every time one of my tagged sharks was found, I received something in the mail, showing the card that I had filled out indicating the length, the fork length, the sex, the condition of the fish, and, of course, the location.

These are cool little tags. They are a piece of monofilament with a really sharp point on one end that you place in a slot on a metal poker, and the monofilament goes up to a little plastic capsule with a very secret-looking little message rolled up in a scroll that fits into this capsule at the top. It has a neoprene screw top on it that makes it somewhat waterproof, and all this information's written on this waterproof scroll. It says, "Please contact the Narragansett Lab of the National Marine Fisheries Service."

I had sharks that swam to and were caught in Mexican waters. I had sharks that swam to South Africa. Tiger sharks just go all over the place, especially the bigger ones. I got tag reports up and down Florida where sharks that I caught and tagged were caught a week later. Fish don't stop eating. It was fun. I had tagged sharks that swam up the coast and were caught in New England, and I think I had one that made it up into Nova Scotia.

LAST MANGO

I had some problems with the boat when I first got it. It caught on fire. The *Last Mango* was built, brand-new, for me in Maine. By the time it was ready for delivery it was too late in the winter to bring it down by sea, so I had them put it on a truck and ship it to Daytona. From Daytona I took it to Vero.

I had a lot of work to do on it to turn it into a fishing boat. We were running it down in the ocean, and I was just offshore of Cape Canaveral when I stepped on one of the Freeman deck hatches. I was barefoot and burned my foot when I stepped on the hatch. When I lifted the hatch, smoke billowed out, and I thought that my brand-new boat was going to burn down before I ever got to fish it.

When the smoke cleared a little bit, I was able to look down there but did not see flames. We got a fire extinguisher, reached down inside, and just shot it all over. It turned out that the dry-exhaust stack had been installed less than half an inch underneath the deck cowlings and was wrapped with one layer of very thin fiberglass insulation tape.

When I called up the boat manufacturer, one of the most successful boat builders in Maine, I said, "Gosh, you're not going to believe this, but the exhaust was installed half an inch below the deck supports and they caught on fire."

His words were: "Ayeup; that's the way we build 'em up heyuh."

That was it. No apology; no nothing. Tough luck, buddy! Better just take your new boat and patch it up yourself.

Well, we did, and it was major surgery. We had to cut out the exhaust from under the deck and drop it down a few more inches away from the deck. That gave us room to wrap it with insulation more seriously. I put a one-inch blanket of fireproof, heat-resistant foam on it and then wrapped it with three layers of heavier tape and added a coating of fire-resistant mastic.

You would have thought anybody who fishes a boat knows you don't go out to sea with a fire hazard looming in the near future. With a certain amount of coaxing, the boat builder eventually made good on the expenses, and then some.

BALES

I saw lots of bales [of marijuana] and went by them all. Those were the "pirate days" for some in the fishing world. I can remember going down to the fish house and just trying not to look. There were big boats and people busy doing something around big semis [laughs]. Maybe I shouldn't be saying that, but it's common knowledge to many. Everybody heard the stories; I just happened to get a bird's-eye view. It felt like I was in a potentially dicey situation, but I never paid it much attention. I just wanted to get to my boat and go fishing.

CHARTER FISHING THE NEW *MANGO*

As a charter captain, I'm a newcomer on the block. Captain Glenn Cameron was "the man" and couldn't have been nicer when I showed up with the refurbished *Last Mango*. He put in a good word for me at the Fort Pierce City Marina when I was having difficulty renting a slip. Much of what I do today is based on paying close attention to Glenn, but there's no substitute for going out there and doing it.

I've been a charter captain for five years, and a very important aspect of the charter business is being able to keep people interested in enjoying their day and communicate with them in between whatever action comes your way. My son, who mated for me for a couple years, used to entertain them better than I did. When I was busy, that responsibility would fall to him. One of the things he said was, "You know, fishing is hours of boredom punctuated by moments of sheer mayhem."

And that's pretty much what charter fishing can be. There are times when there is a pause in the action, and that's when good conversation comes into play. Everyone loves to talk about fishing, no matter where you go or who you're with. If it's on the boat, talking to customers, or somewhere at a party, the conversation always gets around to fishing stories.

BIG DOLPHIN

That sixty-two-pound dolphin [mahimahi] was a big catch. We had some exceptional dolphin fishing in the spring of 2008 and caught four fish between forty-seven and sixty-two pounds that season. The sixty-two-pounder was caught by my friend Patrick, an airline pilot who had come here from Hawaii to go fishing on the *Mango*.

It was a little sloppy that day, and I suggested that they take Dramamine the night before the trip. They insisted that airline pilots didn't worry about being seasick, and they were half right. We weren't in the ocean more than forty minutes [laughs] when Patrick's buddy started heavin' over the side.

People try to hide it, of course, at first. They really fight it, and you can't blame them. It's a bad feeling. But eventually it gets them. It certainly does. He was down for the count when we put a couple live baits out and trolled across the bar.

It was the beginning of June, and the dolphin bite had tapered off to nothing. We were looking for a kingfish bite on our live bait. As I turned to go back over the ledge, one line came out of the release clip and the reel was screaming. You could tell it was a big fish. We saw it jumping in the air as it beelined south on light drag.

As I turned the boat to chase down this monster, another line went off, and we had two on. We jammed the drag up tight on the smaller fish, thinking it would break off and we could focus on the monster that Patrick had on his line.

Amazingly, the smaller fish, a twenty-seven-pounder, came right to the boat and was in the box before it knew what was going on, and it was definitely time to focus on the largest dolphin I had ever seen. This fish had almost spooled us, and we chased him down with no uncertain effort to get some line back on the reel. The battle took some time, with Patrick doing his part and the fish slowly tiring, or so we thought.

For the last hour of this fish's life, he was fifteen feet straight down under the boat and turned sideways, as dolphin do, to create the most resistance and tension on the line, knots, and hook. You couldn't budge him without taking the chance of breaking the twenty-pound test.

Patrick was in good shape. He was a big, strong, strapping twenty-eight-year-old guy with good technique. That's not always the situation on a charter. With one man down and no mate that day, the gaff shot became a little tricky. The fish was stubborn and knew all the tricks. We had well over an hour invested in this fight and didn't want to screw it up now. There are plenty of big dolphin lost at this critical point. I would maneuver the boat for a decent gaff shot, and in the five seconds it took for me to get in position, the fish would ease away just out of range. He was one smart fish.

So I gaffed him off the stern with a great gaff shot. At last, I'm going to get this sucker in the boat. I couldn't lift him. It's not like an axe handle on a kingfish. It was a long skinny gaff, and I just tried to lift him straight up.

We were all exhausted from standing in the sun fighting this fish. So we opened the stern to pull in a sixty-pound fish. It was a narrow-gauge gaff, and I didn't want to take the chance of having it come off. When I did gaff him, he never even moved. He had given it his all, right to the end. Guess his time was up. Once I realized just how big he was, I thought I'll just slide him in the door, and I did. We captured him.

We caught a fifty-two-pounder on a charter. And a young man caught that. It was pretty exciting. When we kingfish, we use live bait. It's unique, because there's two different ways that you could catch kingfish. The traditional method is trolling with dead ballyhoo. That's what a lot of people think of as trolling or deep-sea fishing.

In the summer in Fort Pierce, the water clears up and calms down, and the most effective way to catch a fish is by slow trolling or drifting live bait. The tackle that we use for live bait is dictated by the size of the bait. Three of the most common live-bait fish are sardines, cigar minnows, and threadfin herring. They all get lumped in as the same generic term for bait fish, but they're all such a small size that the best way to fish them is with light tackle.

Typically, you put small hooks in them that won't damage them so that when you troll them, they'll stay alive. You troll them slowly because otherwise you would drown them. You have to be able to troll it somewhere around 1.8 to 2 knots, and it's critical to keep the bait alive. You hook them through the nostrils, and that allows them to swim. To be an effective bait, the fish has to stay alive. Trolling slowly allows them to still breathe and swim. You want the bait back there swimming and looking as natural as it can possibly be, so we use very light tackle and a light wire leader with small hooks on it.

Use a stinger rig for most of your trolling, which catches better and allows you to catch a kingfish, which typically nips the back half of your bait that's hooked only through the nose. So you have a trailing hook that goes three-quarters of the way down the bait and just trails back there. You catch your fish more often on that. The trailing hook is wired to the first hook.

When you battle these fish, you can't bear down on them. It's not like catching a grouper or an amberjack or even most of the fishing you do in the river, because there you have a larger hook and a heavier leader in most cases. When you're live-baiting in the ocean and trolling for kingfish and catch a thirty-pound kingfish, you've got four-pound wire leader attached to a swivel that's just barely big enough to see. The stealth factor is significant here, especially with kingfish, because their eyesight is so good. If you put out a bigger leader and a bigger hook, you won't catch him. No science there.

Although there is that interesting thing about rods and cones in a kingfish's eye. Kingfish and wahoo bite at daylight and near dark. I think it's because the rods and cones adapt to the change in light more quickly than the bait fish. They have a distinct advantage in the morning of seeing what they're doing and attacking that bait fish, which doesn't see as well, because it doesn't have the sophistication in its eyesight to adjust to the light.

The big kingfish is quite similar to the dolphin story, because you have light tackle. To protect the small leader, the four-pound leader, and the twenty-pound monofilament line, you can't force the fish in. Finesse is everything. The hardest thing to teach people who are trying to learn to fish in this situation is to develop their technique, not to waste their energy. You can wind on that reel all day long, and nothing's going to happen because the drag's so light. No line's going to come in. If you have the clicker on, it sounds like something's going on, but all you're doing is making noise.

So the most important thing that I tell anglers who are searching for a better technique is to use the rod to catch the fish and the reel to store the line. And that wraps it up. The explanation for that is exactly how fishing rods are designed. You pull up on the rod delicately and bring the fish that much closer to the boat, then you drop your rod tip slowly, not allowing any slack to get in the line, and wind that line onto the spool as you drop your rod tip. Do that repeatedly and that's the best technique for fishing. Whoever's running the boat can aid in that by giving the angler less resistance by backing down on the fish or chasing the fish.

AN OCEAN SUNFISH

We caught that and kept it in a tank. We kept the mola mola alive, and I was in touch with Sea World by phone that day. We were actually looking for juvenile dusky sharks for them, and I thought the mola mola might be a cool thing for them to have in their tank.

They checked back with headquarters and sent a semitruck-trailer with a huge tank of filtered saltwater just for live fish. It was parked in my parking lot next to the boat for the sharks that I was catching. This was in Daytona, Ponce Inlet. We had arranged this the year before, and I had taken such good records of what I caught that I learned

Mola mola, an ocean sunfish. One of the strangest fish in the Atlantic, it also grows to be one of the biggest and heaviest, living mainly on jellyfish.

that the shark migration was so predictable, it was scary. So I knew that there were juvenile dusky sharks that came through just south of Ponce Inlet around the first two weeks of March.

I coordinated this all with Sea World and worked with them on it. They showed up the last day of those two weeks that I told them that the sharks would be there. We had some lousy weather, and all the conditions had changed. The dusky sharks were gone. The people from Sea World show up with this big, expensive operation and [laughs] this truck and tank. The best thing I caught all day was that mola mola. I thought, well, heck, maybe that'll be something that will make them feel like they didn't waste their time completely. We fished for them for three or four days anyway, but I knew that it was too late to catch dusky sharks. Anyway, they didn't want the mola mola. We threw it back, and we threw it back alive.

FIVE-HUNDRED-POUND GOLIATH GROUPER

This is a five-hundred-pound gutted goliath grouper. We got him in the boat through the door in the back, and there was no way to unload him. There's no handles on a five-hundred-pound grouper. So we found some old wood and built a ramp [laughs]. We attached a big line to the grouper and used a truck in the parking lot to tow him out of the boat onto the dock.

A tow truck was needed to move this 500-pound grouper from boat to dock.

CHARTER FISHING

What I really like about the charter fishing business is the challenge. It's so different from commercial fishing. A commercial fisherman leads a very solitary existence, where he spends all of his time in the ocean. It's hard to have friends other than the other fishermen. Kingfishing consisted of early mornings (kings bite best at first light), long days (there is also a good bite just before dark), unloading your catch at the fish house, catching or buying bait for the next day, and finding your way home for a late dinner only to get up and do it again. Longer trips offshore are less frantic, but you are still away from home too much.

Captain Tris Colket at his home in Fort Pierce. For Tris, one of the hardest things about being a commercial fisherman was being away from home so much.

It can be hard on a marriage and a family. I missed taking my kids to Little League games and participating in their development.

Charter days can be long but are generally less strenuous. Meeting people from varied backgrounds is a treat after thirty some years of hard-core kingfishing, swordfishing, shark-, and tilefishing.

The boat project, fixing the *Mango* up, was extremely therapeutic for me, because my son came back from where he was working and worked with me on that. So it was a chance to redeem myself in some ways and get to know him better. He was in his mid-twenties and had been working as a stockbroker and stuck in a place that he didn't like. He called me up to see what I thought about whether he should stick it out or not.

Having always worked for myself and having never been afraid to break out and try something different, I said, "If you're not happy, come on back here, and I just happen to have a project I'm involved in that will support you for a while and be fun."

So we converted the *Last Mango* from a shark-fishing boat to a charter boat, which I think is one of the most beautiful charter boats out there. I get compliments all the time. There are not many people that walk down the dock and don't recognize the uniqueness of it. It's hard to imagine that we could have transformed a commercial boat into the boat that it is now.

A WONDERFUL DAY

Warren Kremmin called me one day in early summer of 2011 to inquire about a fishing charter for his family. Warren wanted the "perfect fishing day" for his wife and two daughters so that their introduction to the world of offshore fishing would lay the groundwork for future fishing trips. The forecast was good and sea conditions ideal, so I told him that we could make it all happen for them . . . well, after all, that's what we do!

As is often the case, just catching our live bait for the day is a pretty big thrill for first-timers, and when we used that bait to catch them some nice big kingfish, it was apparent that I had accomplished my mission. They were stoked.

We moved on to a spot where we catch grouper and amberjack, and the bite was hot. With the help of my first mate, Devin, two forty-pound amberjack were in the boat in short order, and each of the young girls had caught the biggest fish they had ever seen.

When it was finally time for Dad to enter the fray, the girls were pretty worn out. We drifted over the same spot in about 160 feet of water, and his rod tip twitched for a second before bending in half and almost pulling him to his knees. Two hours later, after a tag-team effort with his wife, Erika, Warren landed the biggest amberjack I had ever seen on the deck of the *Mango*. It was way too big for our fish box, so we pulled him into the shade and kept him coved with a wet towel on the way back to the dock, where the City Marina's digital scale documented the official weight at 101.7 pounds.

I think that day was the perfect trip for them. Warren, it turned out, knew a little more about fish than our average charter. He is part owner

This 101.7-pound amberjack made for the Kremmins'"perfect fishing day."

in Blue Ribbon Seafood, a major player at New York's Fulton Fish Market. I guess he had one hell of a good fish story to tell when they got home.

THE PEOPLE

What I didn't expect and what I really like about charter fishing are the people. Ninety-nine percent of them are kind, interesting, appreciative, and fun. They are what makes it really enjoyable.

2

Captain A. J. Brown

To hear A. J. [Addi James] Brown's slow, deep Virginia drawl was always a pleasure. I thought his voice was what a Confederate general might have sounded like. A. J. Brown was renowned as a superb and skilled commercial kingfisherman, but fishing was only one of his talents. He was an expert welder, golfer, pool player, diver, gambler, and day trader on the stock market.

When he kindly allowed me to interview him for this book in late summer of 2009, A. J. had just been diagnosed with incurable throat cancer and had been given six months to live. He died a little more than six months later.

As a fisherman, A. J. followed the king mackerel up and down Florida's east coast. His life was marked by consistently huge catches, as well as some unexpected calamities. He learned from the misadventures and became better as a result. He was highly respected and had many friends. By the time his life abruptly ended, A. J. Brown had become one of Florida's most respected commercial king mackerel captains. This is his story.

A. J. Brown in His Own Words

I was born on October 23, 1947, in Halifax, Virginia. I grew up on a tobacco farm. My family still farms in that area. We had, I guess, probably about 250 acres.

My dad liked to fish, but all we used was cane poles. We had a bundle of cane poles about as big around as a basketball. We had tenant farmers on the farm, and every Saturday they would take sort of a break with my dad, and we'd go to the river and go fishing with the cane poles. There'd be twenty or thirty poles there, and I loved it. In fact, when I was a little boy, my dad would sometimes go fishing with

A. J. Brown on his boat, *Second Wind*.

his buddies, and he'd leave me home. I slept through and would miss the trip. I was just five or six at the time. So I tied a string to him while he was asleep and then tied the string to me. When he woke up and got out of bed, he woke me up, so he had to take me with him fishing.

Fishing, I loved it, I don't know why. I was always addicted to it. Even when I would ride across a river I was trying to figure out some way I could go fishing in it. I think that was the James River, up in Virginia. We caught catfish and bream mostly. We didn't target the carp. It's not a very good eating fish. The big thing for Dad was having his buddies come and go fishing for catfish. That's what they liked to do most of all was catch catfish.

I grew up with the tenant-farm kids. They lived in the old family house down on the farm, and we had a big pond. The old colored matriarch [Lucille] fished in that pond about every day. We swam and did everything with those kids. I did have two older sisters.

LUCILLE

A funny story. It's not that she didn't love them, but Lucille had a lot of kids, and they were around my age. One was named Frog, one was named Tadpole, and she had a girl named Puttsy and one named Buttons and Bows. I grew up with them, and they just treated me like family, and I was family.

My dad was farming when I was young, and me and those kids played in the pond and ran together and climbed trees, everything. It was quite an experience. Their mother was the matriarch. I think she had sixteen or seventeen children. She had a big ol' goiter. But she was a mamma hen, you know.

When I was in my twenties, I went back up there and went to this country store and saw her, And I said, "Hi, Lucille."

She said, "Who are you?"

And I said, "I'm Jimmy."

She said, "My baby!" She had boobs out to here, you know those big ol' things. And she just grabbed me up and held me tight. It was quite a moving experience.

But that's who I grew up with mostly, those tenant farmer children. A lot of them didn't ever go to school. That was in the 1950s. School wasn't pursued at the time. It wasn't mandatory. They could have sent 'em, I'm sure, but they didn't.

Lucille had one son named Lennie and one named Big Boy that were my age, and we ran together a lot. Just hunting and carrying on, running up and down the creeks. It was a great childhood. I thought it was rough at the time, but as I look back on it, it was great.

CATFISH

We caught mostly catfish with cane poles. Catfish will bite about anything. When we were fishing with the cane poles on the bank, we used worms mostly. Chicken guts was very, very good bait for catfish. We had chickens on the farm. In fact, I got my butt whipped there.

I had my fishing pole down by the pond, baited it, and laid it down when one of Lucille's ducks came around and swallowed the bait on the fishing pole. The next thing I know, the duck is flying around on the end of my fishing pole. The hook was down his throat. They ended up eating that duck [laughs].

CLEANING AND COOKING CATFISH

Dad had a nail on the smokehouse. In fact, he had a couple of them. He'd take a catfish, stick his head up on that nail, and make a couple of slices on each side, and then take the pliers and pull the skin off. Skin it down, just cut the head off and gut it. He could clean them fast. If it was small, we cooked the whole fish. That's the best way and my favorite way. When they get big, you fillet them. My dad was an amazing cook and made a lot of catfish stews, which were unbelievably good. He was the cook for the Masonic Lodge, and he was always cooking something there. Deep-fried whole catfish was my favorite. They're delicious.

THE HOME FARM

We sold the farm that we grew up on because none of us were there. I wish we hadn't, but we did. It went to one of my neighbors' son that Dad was real close to, and he still farms it. The rest of my family is still in farming. They got a lot of land, and they still do real well. It's amazing, but they still farm tobacco. They raise other crops, too, like corn, wheat, everything else. But tobacco's the staple.

TELEPHONE FISHING

Telephone fishing, of course, is illegal. The Ogeechee River, which flows down into the Savannah, is one of the prettiest rivers. It's weird how it flows almost north instead of south. It flows up like an upstream river and is very pristine. They don't let any boat with above a 10-horsepower motor on it, and you have to go over logs.

My friend had an old army telephone, and we had him in the front boat with his wife, and she'd have a net. We'd be in the back boat behind them. They used johnboats, because you can go over logs and branches. When you crank that thing [the telephone], it sends an electric current to the bottom, and it affects the whiskers on the catfish. They run to the top and go crazy. I mean, they are all over the place. You can dip them up and put them in the boat and, frankly, we had a lot of fun doing it.

VIETNAM

You know, of course, when I was a teenager, I had other things on my mind than fishing [laughs]. I went to Vietnam when I was eighteen, right after high school, and stayed in the army three years. Vietnam was a trip.

I was fortunate. I was a helicopter repair specialist. I even had a job as a bartender at the Officer's Club at night. So I had it pretty good there, to tell you the truth. But I lost some good friends.

Vietnam was, for a young man, a growing experience, going from high school to Vietnam and being brainwashed by the government. They'd tell you all the propaganda about what they believed was wrong and how you were supposed to react to the war. It was more of a political war than anything else. They wanted a head count just to show that they were doing something. But they never did actually try to win the war. They just farted around, mainly. Body count was all they wanted.

I tended bar there mostly for helicopter pilots. I was in the Helicopter Division, 321 Aviation Division. And it was, in fact, the same division that Lieutenant Calley was in. He got caught and blamed for killing all those people in My Lai in '68, '69. The My Lai Massacre was right out of Chu Lai. But civilians got killed all the time.

Like I said, the warrant officers would come in overnight, and the main thing they wanted was a head count . . . people dead. And they'd say, "We killed some gooks today, and we don't know whether they were bad or good." And they'd write it all up. That was a head count. It really affected you in a lot of hard ways.

I was fortunate. I didn't have to fight much. We were under constant barrage from incoming shells, but I never actually had to go out in the bush and fight. It was still a wakeup call for me.

That Lieutenant Calley just got caught with his hands in the kitty. In the army, if something bad happens, somebody's going to pay whether he's guilty or not. And he paid. They knew people were getting killed all the time. But you have to also look at it another way, because I know quite a few instances where the guys would be holed up around a base, and some kid would run in there with a bomb and blow himself up. So it was especially hard, like I said, when you're eighteen years old, and they train you to kill. That's why so many people from the Vietnam and the Iraqi war have so much trouble adjusting when they get back. They're so young, and then they go through that stuff, and then they're screwed up for the rest of their life.

One of the boys from my hometown that I hadn't seen very much made his whole tour of duty and was flying out, leaving the base that morning. They shot him down on his trip home. He didn't die immediately, but he had severe burns. He made it to Fort Hood, Texas, and died there.

But, yeah, over there, it's best not to become too good a friend because everything goes so crazy. It was just a crazy place to be. Some of the guys couldn't give a damn. They teach you propaganda and all the stuff about kill-kill-kill the enemy. It's gung-ho from the time you hit basic training until you get over there.

CAVE KILLERS

Some of the smaller guys would go right down in those cave holes after the Vietcong, and a lot of them got killed. Some of them made it, but I don't know how. They had big gonads to do it, I know that. But I knew some of them, and when those guys came in out of the bush after two or three months, they were a crazy bunch. They'd settle down after a while. In the tunnels you can't carry a rifle; you'd have to go with a .45 revolver and a knife. Most of them put the knife right in their teeth. They had underground bunkers way up under there. It was unbelievable.

I would say Vietnam was a wasted war. It was terrible, and it was bad for a lot of people. It ruined a lot of people's lives and never accomplished a doggoned thing. We just walked away and never tried to win. They could have won but never pushed it. It was a political war.

And I rebelled against it as soon as I got home. But anyway, that's another story. No, I never participated in demonstrations. I didn't go that far. I know we got treated badly. In fact, when I got home, I still had a little less than a year left, and we were treated so badly here that I signed up and went to Germany. I spent my last six, eight months in Germany, because we were treated terrible here. People would spit on you and just treated you like a dog.

RAMBLING

Once I got back and away from that crap over there is when I rebelled against all of it. I thought it was terrible, so I was a hippie for a while [laughs]. I traveled, rambled a lot, and went to work at Myrtle Beach. I worked at Myrtle Beach for a long time. That's where I met my wife. I actually worked as a mate on a charter boat. It was pretty good. I didn't like dealing with the people, the customers, you know. A lot of them were drunks and thought they knew everything. They'd tell you how to fish. They'd say, "We're not catching anything; we need to move."

Later, when I first moved here, I worked with the *Little George*, a charter boat right out of Fort Pierce. But in any charter boat business you got to put up with the customers. That is why I love kingfishing so much. There is such freedom, without having to deal with anybody else.

PIPE FITTER

I became a pipe welder and got into the pipe-fitters' union in Augusta, Georgia. At the time, the nuclear plants were springing up everywhere. I worked at the Department of Energy for a while where they made the A-bomb. I think that's where they made bombs, so we called it the "bomb plant." I got to be a pretty good welder, and I started traveling. I went to Mississippi and Alabama working on nuke plants. It was through the pipe-fitters' Local 150 out of Augusta. They arranged the jobs, and you'd go hire on. That paid real well, and I traveled around doing that for about twenty years.

I was working at a nuclear plant in New Orleans when a friend of mine called me. He knew how much I liked to fish and liked the ocean. He called me and said, "You need to get down here. You won't ever leave."

You know, I laughed at him at the time, but I came down here, I think it was in 1980, and I never left.

ST. LUCIE NUCLEAR POWER PLANT

I worked all over the St. Lucie Nuclear Plant. Mostly, I was a pipe fitter and welder. But I worked down around the intake. I'll get in trouble here [laughs].

The intake is at the back of the plant, where all the canals feed in. Underneath there was a mezzanine. There's so much paperwork involved in making a nuclear pipe weld, and sometimes I'd make tacks in the weld, and then I'd go for two days waiting for something to do. Under the mezzanine, you could see the snapper and snook and everything else down there, and we'd take hand lines for catching those things.

I never will forget, the superintendent was right up above, looking out there one day. I had thrown my line out, and a snook grabbed it and jumped and did a big ol' flip in there. He [the superintendent] said,

"What was that?" [laughs]. I turned the line loose and let the fish go. I didn't want to fight 'em there. But that was amazing.

That's where the water comes into the cooling part of the plant, runs through to cool it, and then it pushes it back outside the plant, creating those boils in the ocean just off the beach from the plant. The warm water is the reason that's such a good fishing area. I used to pompano fish down there all the time. There was a road right by the plant, and you could go all the way to the beach and walk down and cast out. That was great pompano fishing, and when we finished these plants here, I didn't want to move.

KINGFISHING

So I met Wild Bill Hodges. I didn't know it at the time, but he was from Virginia. Wild Bill and I grew up not far from each other. He traveled a lot, and he would let me fish his boat when he was gone. I went with him fishing to start with, to sort of learn it. And then one summer, I was still doing what we call "refueling outages." It is where we'd go in for two months, and you'd work seven- to thirteen-hour days, and then you're off. And you draw unemployment or draw something. And then I'd have three or four months until I started fishing with Bill on his boat.

Bill went to Alaska for quite a while, and he let me use the boat. Bill was a good fisherman, and he was a good teacher. I started fishing his boat, and that's when I learned. I was as lost as last year's Easter eggs most of the time there at the start, but he gave me the basics. I remember going out there in the fleet and everybody yelling at me because I was running through the middle of them. I'd see somebody catching fish and run over to them and try to get as close as I could.

Of course, they were yelling at me, "Small ocean, ain't it?" and stuff like that [laughs]. So, anyway, I got to the point that I thought I could make a living at it, not a very good living, but a living. But I love it so much. So I bought my first boat. And that was the *Playboy*.

THE *PLAYBOY*

It was a 24-foot Stapleton. It's the boat that blew out the windows when Eddie Black had it. It had a gas engine, and when he cranked it up, some fumes in there blew the windows out over at Riverside Marina. It blew his fish box, too, loaded with sixteen hundred pounds of kingfish, up onto the stern. I wasn't there. I just heard tales of it. He was fortunate. Yep, that was the boat I later bought. That was a great fishing boat, and it was a good, seaworthy boat for a 24-footer.

I forgot what I named the thing. But that was originally the *Playboy*. I think I painted it a different name. I got where I didn't want a name on it because we fished all up through the Cape, and I didn't want to have to put up with somebody yelling at me over the radio. I wanted to be incognito. I'd say that was in about '85, or somewhere in the '80s.

I still worked the outages at the power plant every once in a while if I needed the money bad enough, because the money was so good. I could work two months and make about $15,000 or better, and that was good at the time. That carried me through, because I wasn't that good a fisherman then.

As you well know, it takes a while to get it. But I loved it. It was a sense of independence that I don't think many people ever have. To go out there, go out in the ocean, and if you don't want to turn on your radio, don't want to listen to anybody all day, you don't have to, and you don't have to answer to anybody. To me that's being superindependent. The freedom means more to me than anything.

I started traveling [up and down the Florida coast] pretty soon. Back then the fishing was plentiful. There were a lot of fish, and we didn't have borders. And you could still make a fairly decent living by fishing right out of here without traveling too far.

KINGFISH NETS

The kingfish nets weren't that bad at first. The drift nets weren't as bad at first either. And that's another reason I left, because they don't drift them up there [at the Cape] as much. They can't, because of the Cape Canaveral Shoals.

The circle nets were bad. I mean, they were awful destructive. They had such a drop out of the center of them, plus the fish were always in terrible shape. I remember, it got to the point where you had to dodge drift nets to get to the offshore bar. Then you knew you were screwed, because the fish were spooked as hell from dodging nets all night. I'm pretty sure that's when I started traveling.

Tommy Jones and George Kaul were still traveling, and Tommy and I became friends. Tommy is a very good fisherman. He still tilefished a lot, but he got into the kingfishing, and then he and I became traveling buddies, which was good, because Tommy introduced me to a lot of people that I didn't know, and I became friends with a lot of Sebastian boys and the Cape Canaveral and Daytona fishermen. As long as you don't tell too much and tell too many other people what's going on, you'll stay on their good side. If you cross them, now, it's Katy bar the door.

So I liked it. I liked traveling. I didn't have any trouble staying out in the ocean at night, and I didn't have a family. I got divorced when I was young, and I had two sons, but they were up in Carolina, and I'd see them there every once in a while. But I loved to fish. I didn't mind staying out in the ocean. I would kingfish all day and bottom-fish at night and go back at it the next day.

Of course, when we were fishing then, there was a lot more fish. The Northeast Grounds of Fort Pierce was about as good as it gets in the winter. But what those drift nets did to those fish was bad. They've just rebounded here in the last five years. About five or six years ago, we started getting our fishery back together. And I've seen more fish in the last two or three years than I've ever seen in my life. I mean huge schools of them, especially in the wintertime. No way in the world that anybody could ever catch them all trolling.

But those drift nets really put a damper on all the king mackerel here. And once that was over, it seemed everybody got out of fishing. That pretty much did us in. At one time we had a huge fleet of boats here. But it dwindled down, and there weren't that many boats left, because you couldn't make a living at it. It was because of those nets. And fortunately, like I said, I still carried my pipe-fitter's book. I've still got it, though I just retired. I still had my pipe-fitter's book, and every once in a while, if I had to, I'd go back and do some welding.

THREE WATERSPOUTS

I'll tell you a funny story. It didn't materialize where it would hurt anybody bad, but it was a bad storm. We were fishing the Pines, up off of Sebastian. I was in shore there. I don't know if you remember or know a guy named Jerry Harrison, but he's Jerry; that's all you could say. But he's gotten to be real religious. So, here we were fishing, and this huge black cloud came and just sort of spread out. It looked really weird, scary. Three waterspouts come down all at once around us. It was scary.

Jerry gets on the radio and says, "All right, boys, that's the Father, Son, and the Holy Ghost. You'd better look out and get your affairs in order" [laughs].

Oh, they were close by. Everybody went to scramblin'. It was sort of funny for him to say that at the time. He said, "You better get your stuff together because they . . ."

BIG STORMS

Another instance, we were fishing on the high bar at Sebastian, which is one of my very favorite places to fish. It's eighteen miles straight out, but what a beautiful set of reefs. It just comes up so high, thirty or forty feet in places. It's a great place for bottom-fish and bait, and mackerel love it there. The fish were biting pretty good.

They said that morning we had till the afternoon before this storm would hit, but about ten o'clock it got deathly still there. And you could look off into the horizon and see a black-like rope, and it just kept getting closer. Everybody started panicking a little bit. It was a prefrontal trough, and it was coming out of the northwest. It was about as hairy a one as I ever saw. When it got to us, it blew 50, 55, and we're eighteen miles out.

The only way you could get back was go toward the northwest. So you had to go into it until you got to the lee of the land, where you could turn and go back toward the inlet a bit without getting swamped. It was that bad. It was at least fifteen-foot waves there and just pounding into it. They lost a couple of boats. And then you had to deal with going into Sebastian Inlet. It was a lot of boats together and it was a real hairy experience. I had that 24 Stapleton. That was like being a cork in a bathtub.

And then we had a lot of bad ones off of Jupiter fishing in the afternoons. I remember very well, Billy Smith, he's a clammer now, but he had somehow got turned in that thing. It was blowing 50 there. He got the cables and everything in his wheel, so he couldn't steer. So he was just fighting it into the storm.

Then we fished off Daytona. Daytona is a whole different ball game. There's so much area there. The storms in the afternoon there are horrible. In fact, that's one of the places where Al Tyrrell got struck by lightning.[1] If you spent the night out there, you had to deal with the storms

---

1 In *Great Kingfish Captains* by Terry Howard, Al Tyrrell tells about being struck by lightning off of Daytona.

in the afternoon, and that was part of it, you know. If you couldn't do it, then there wasn't any need in going out there. You couldn't make it just a one-day trip, in and out. It's just too far.

I spent so much time in the boat, and I loved it. I read books on navigation. I even wanted to try to use a sextant, because it just fascinated me that the mariners used to travel with a sextant and the stars. The stars and the ocean always fascinated me. That was a lot of fun learning that ocean and learning how to use that sextant. But I guess if you do anything long enough, you get familiar with it.

HITTING THE JETTY

This is a good story. It was back when we could still net pogies. I was up the river and threw out my gill net, but I didn't hurry, and it got loaded with pogies. I threw out the net and then had to rope it back in, it had so many of them in it. And I laid it in the stern of the boat back there and took off running in this real dark night. I had the autopilot on, an old Benmar pilot, and every once in a while that doggoned thing would go out. I thought I cleared that inlet, and I put that pilot on, and I went back to the stern to try to get my pogies out of the net. I wanted to put them on some ice, where they'd stay firm.

Then I felt it [the autopilot] go out. It just turned hard left, and when I get up to the wheel, I hit the north jetty. Just rammed into it and knocked a hole about as big as a basketball in the bow. It hit so hard that it knocked the motor off the mounts, and both exhausts were flooding water in.

Jimmy Reeves and Tommy Feygo were nearby, and Jimmy threw me a rope and pulled on my bow and pulled me back. Tommy Feygo got behind me and pushed. Jimmy pulled me down to Dynamite Point, and Tommy pushed me with his bow up on the sand, where I wouldn't sink. I had cracked two ribs, but I got out and put a rag in that hole and Sea Tow, whoever that is that tows people in, brought pumps over there, and we pumped the water out. They towed it back to the dock. The motor was off the mounts.

I hadn't cleared the inlet. It's deceiving, especially on out the north jetty, because the south jetty comes out shorter. But the north jetty comes out about a hundred feet further. And so it's easy to think you're through.

It was a real dark night, though, and like I said, I was panicking and wanted to get my bait out of the net and on ice. I should have never put it on the pilot. Those Benmar autopilots were famous for doing that, and when they go out every once in a while, they just take a hard right or left turn.

I cracked my ribs on the steering wheel. I went into shock when I first got off the boat at Dynamite Point. The Coast Guard had called the paramedics. They pulled up by me where I was laying on the sandbar, and Fire and Rescue came over, and, thank God, they revived me all right. It scared me so damned bad.

At the dock, the Coast Guard told me, "Get out of the boat," and, you know, let her go sink.

And I said, "No, y'all get me up there on that thing [the boat crane]." So I didn't lose my boat. I didn't have a hell of a lot of money back then.

SIXTY-FIVE-POUND KING MACKEREL

Biggest king mackerel I ever caught was sixty-five pounds. Caught it on an umbrella rig off of Jupiter. And I was using my deck reel, which I fished with a lot. I was trolling real deep, and he hooked on my rig. Of course, the bottom rig [reel] did a lot of the fighting for me till I got him up. Sixty-five-pound kingfish. I had 300-pound mono line.

When it came up, it was a big ol' sow, and she come up to the boat pretty well done. I just had to get her in the boat. That was the biggest king mackerel I've ever seen. I'd caught them in the forties before, but I'd never seen a sixty-five-pounder. That's a big fish. I just gaffed and pulled her over into the boat.

BOTTOM-FISHING

Tommy Jones and I fished for amberjack for a while and caught some close to a hundred pounds. In fact, I caught an amberjack one day and gutted it and was telling Tommy, "Man, look at his belly. It looks funny." So I cut on it. There's a tilefish, three feet long.

We fished right out of here before they closed the Oculina Bank. We'd catch, sometimes, 2,000 pounds of amberjack a day. We used bottom reels. Tommy would fish one side, and I'd fish the other. And we had a reel on each side. You'd get one up and the other one'd let his down while you were coming up. You'd hook 'em—they'd bite that fast. You'd hook up, and he'd be letting his down. It's pretty fast. It's a lot of work, because you got, well, 2,000 pounds, and you got to handle

Back in port, A. J. Brown hoses down *Second Wind* after a big catch.

them about five times. We've had the boat full of fish, throwing them up beside boxes up in the front when they were biting that well.

He and I did a lot of fishing, but we didn't advertise it. We fished for snowy grouper a lot. Tommy knew some wrecks he found when he was tilefishing. And you sure didn't tell anyone else then, because they'd fish it out. Bob Ferber found that great snowy wreck down there they call *The Bar and Grill*. How he found it, I'll never know. But he'd come into Hudgins Fish House every day that he went out, and he'd have four or five hundred of the biggest snowies you could find. And everybody was just foaming at the mouth to find that spot. But Tommy caught Bob Ferber fishing on the wreck, and that was it.

Bobby Christensen had a longline boat at the time, and I think he got a couple thousand pounds of grouper or better the first day. Floated the line—there were so many fish on it, it floated it up. After that, that wreck got fished out, and finally it ended up on the toilet wall at the fish house, the [GPS] numbers to the wreck [laughs]. Yes, it has been fished out, and now it's got so much wire and sinkers and all this stuff on it, you can't even get a bait down. It gets hung up in everything. But that was a great wreck. It was in 300 feet of water.

Then we had two really good wrecks inside the Oculina Bank. Got one of them from General Mills. Gary Mills was always called "The General." I stole one of his wrecks off of him. He kept you jumping. He was always raising hell, but he really let you go. If you get caught, you get caught. Everybody has the numbers for all the wrecks now. Unless you would find one like some of the recent boats that have sunk and find something there.

Tommy was tilefishing, and an airplane crashed close by. In fact, he saved the pilot's life. And he's looked for that airplane for years and years and never found it.

A BAD STORM

No, I've never been hurt by a waterspout. I've always tried to shy away from them. Most of the time, you can dodge 'em, unless they just drop right on you.

That's what happened to Tommy McHale. I was right beside Tommy that day. That's the day he lost his boxes and everything and when his outriggers got down in the wheel. Yeah, that same thing had happened to Billy Stewart. But if you get those outriggers down in there and all that stuff gets locked in your wheel, you're done. I was there that day with Tommy. That was every man for himself, because you couldn't see your arm there beside you, it was so turned up. I was actually trying to troll into it, trying to go forward, and I kept looking at my LORAN, and I was going backwards. It was blowing that hard, it was blowing me in reverse.

BIG CATCHES AND BIG FISH

Unfortunately, when I got into it, it was mostly past the time of big catches. I mean, I had some thousands and fifteen hundreds and stuff like that. I had some real good catches real quick. I remember going to the Pines one morning, and I threw my lines out and didn't have bait on them, just threw them out there. I stopped to put it in a circle on 680 and 015, one of my favorite rocks, and both lines were tight. They had twenty-pounders on each, and I didn't stop pulling. An hour and a half later, I had eighteen hundred pounds. There were fifty fish averaging eighteen to nineteen pounds, and they weighed eighteen hundred and some pounds. A lot of big ones were in there.

We call that the Log Cabin. For some reason, those big fish like to pull in there. I never got any of the really big catches like Steve Lowe or those boys that used to catch all the big catches. You know, after the drift nets, that didn't happen. The drift nets ended all those really big catches.

My fifteen-hundred-pound catch was right up at the Pines. That's one of my very favorite areas, and most of my big catches were there. That's just north of Sebastian Inlet. It runs from about 620 on up to the 700s and inside, that's around the 6,200 line and inshore of it. Right as you get up around 680, there's a lot of rubble and really good bait-holding areas, and that's what we call the Log Cabin, because all the big logs, I mean all the big fish, we pulled out of there. It's nothing in the wintertime to have a twenty-pound average there. Well, the adrenaline gets to running so strong there, when you're pulling big fish, and there's nothing much more fun than to see that line stretch straight out. It's just fantastic.

The ones I like are the wahoos when they stretch them out, but I've lost more than I ever catch. But God knows, I was fishing there north of the Snapper Rock in Fort Pierce, right close to Roger's Rock, where Roger Farlowe used to fish. Anyway, I got that thing on, and it stretched straight out. I mean, it looked, that outrigger was like that [A. J. holds his arm straight out]. And, good Lord, what could this be? And I got him up there, and I know that fish weighed 120 or better. I didn't even try to boat him. That wahoo looked that big around [A. J. holds his arms out]. I didn't even try. I just cut the wire and let him go. I didn't try to hook [gaff] him. No. That thing would have eaten me alive.

Tommy Jones had eighty stitches from one of those things. They open their mouth and are hard to pull. But when they come in the boat, they'll bite you. Yeah, they damn sure will. And their teeth were sharper than the Kings', for some reason. They're just a bit longer. The snout's longer, too. Well, you know, we've all gotten bit. All you got to do is graze your arm.

STRANGE HAPPENINGS

I can tell you about a strange light once. I was leaving Sebastian Inlet there, early one morning, and they fired a rocket from the Cape. There were a lot of small, low clouds coming through at the time. Al Tyrrell calls 'em "spuds." There was a lot of light when that thing came by, and it made just perfect rings of every color. It was one of the most phenomenal things I ever saw in my life. There was every color of the rainbow, ring-ring-ring, right after it went through. That was one of the very coolest things I've ever seen in my life.

I'll tell you something, man. I don't know if you want to put this in the book or not, but it was weird, and it actually happened to me, and I've thought about it a million times. It happened twice in my life.

My son died. I was fishing out here on the Northeast Grounds, and there was a presence in that boat, and I'll swear it to the day I die. There was a presence in that boat with me, and I could feel it.

A few years later, my sister died, and the next week after she died, there was a presence in that boat with me. And I swear to God, it was just like somebody got on there and was standing there looking at me. It scared me in a little way, but that actually happened. That's the honest-to-God truth.

What that means, I have no idea, but it sure happened. I wouldn't tell you just for the hell of it, you know. That happened.

NEAR-SINKINGS

When I hit the jetties, the boat stuck right there. Jimmy Reeves backed me off enough where he could grab a rope and pull the bow around off the rocks. I couldn't do anything. I had no power. He pulled me down there. I was sinking at the time. It was going down. If I hadn't had a wall between the motor and the bow, it would have sunk right then, but that bulkhead saved me from sinking.

I had another close one while leaving the dock at Tommy Jones's. If you come out of there from Tommy's dock and you cut too close, there's a railroad tie that sticks up. I thought I had just run on the gravel, but that railroad tie got caught on my spray rail and pushed a hole in the bow. That was my new boat, the *Second Wind*. I got out almost to the end of the slow zone, and I looked, and the whole cabin was full of water up to the bulkhead. So I turned and went back to the sandbar at Dynamite Point to keep from sinking. I did that same damn thing. Fortunately, it didn't hurt my motor. But that's my two near-sinking experiences.

DIVING TRAGEDY

Far as helping somebody, well, I didn't really help. This was my experience with Dwight Blackwelder. Dwight, Tommy Jones, and another friend, Eric Winterstein, and me were diving, and Dwight had gone down. He was one of the best divers anywhere around here. This was the mini-season for lobster in '07.

Dwight was unbelievable. I could stay down thirty minutes, and Dwight'd stay an hour and a half on one tank of air. But it always scared you to death. And most of the time it was flat, and you could see bubbles. We had a buoy, just one man down at a time, and we followed the buoy as he moved so we'd be right there if he popped up. I watched the bubbles for an hour . . . an hour fifteen . . . an hour twenty. I said, "Holy shit." I was the next diver to go down.

The bubbles were just a little blip, a little teeny thing. I had a feeling. I put my stuff on and went down there and saw his spear gun, which he would never lay down. He always carried it with him. Then I saw Dwight, and he was in a fetal position, just like in his mother's womb. I went over and hooked his arm and vest through this shoulder [points to his right shoulder], put air in my BC [buoyancy compensator], and came up to the boat with him.

At the time, he had a pacemaker, and we thought we heard heartbeats, although we shouldn't, because there was red foam coming out of his mouth. So we tried everything. We knew CPR. We called the Coast Guard, and they met us halfway. But that was the biggest tragedy I've ever experienced. It was a wakeup call there for all of us. I know I've not dove into deep waters much since then, and Tommy hasn't dove any since. Tommy had the bends one time, too. He quit all of it.

COOL DIVING

What was cool about diving was while you were fishing for king mackerel, especially the Northeast Grounds in the 360s and -70s and -80s, you got where you knew what to look for as far as rocks for lobster diving, and you'd write them down. Then Tommy Jones and I would fish till about noon, and I'd throw the anchor on my boat and get on the boat with him. Then I'd jump down and see what was there. You learn the rocks and know what it looked like where you were fishing. We had a lot of fun with that. You'd actually see what you'd been fishing on all of those years.

It's like that Snapper Rock. Boy, that thing's amazing, it's so huge. It's unbelievable the way it twists and turns. There's lots of barracuda there and about everywhere you go. It's amazing you don't catch more than you do. There's 'cudas everywhere. Yeah, you heard Steve Lowe tell stories about when they fished there. They said at one time, it was covered with red snapper.

LOST DIVER

There's another dive story with Jeff Schorner. We kingfished in the morning. We'd done it once before, I think, and did pretty good. I anchored my boat, took my gear, and got on Jeff's boat with him. So I made a dive, got some lobsters, and it was his turn.

We saw this squall away to the west, but it looked like it was slow-moving. We thought we had plenty of time. But he got down, and I was following him around. All you can do is follow these bubbles. It was flat calm, and then that thing came.

It was probably a prefrontal trough. It's one of the most dangerous things you can experience, a prefrontal before a bad low pressure. That thing got there, and it was blowing 20, 25. Once you get that, you can't see, you can't see anything. And I looked and looked, and I knew it was time for him to be up, so I got scared. I figured he'd be up and just drifting. So I called the Coast Guard and said, "Mayday, mayday! I got a diver down!" And they come back, wanted the location and everything.

We were on the VHF, and I was telling all that, and it got out on 19. His wife, unfortunately, had 19 dialed in at their house. So I was telling Tommy Jones, in a nearby boat, I said, "Come over here and help me look. Help me find Jeff."

But anyway, Jeff's wife was listening. Needless to say, that was my last dive trip with Jeff. He got out of king-mackerel fishing not long after that.

Anyway, we were looking, looking, looking, and Jeff had swum to my boat, which was anchored. And he got on my boat and got on the radio and said, "A. J., A. J.!"

I said, "Where the hell are you, Jeff?"

He said, "I'm on your boat."

I say, "Thank God!" [laughs].

My boat was downstream, downcurrent. I'm sure he popped up, saw what was happening, and saw my boat and figured he'd better aim for it. You don't want to try to swim upcurrent. We were lucky. But it was a tide that sort of pushed him that way for a little while, as it usually does. I thought sure he was a goner. He just was fortunate enough to see the boat. And then, after that trough ran through, it got calm.

FOURTEEN-POUND TROUT

See that big trout on the wall? We fished across from the Little Jim [in Fort Pierce], where the boat ramp is, and right in the middle is a really gravelly area. At the first of the incoming tide, you could bounce your shrimp through there and just catch a lot of big trout.

We were fishing, and this is the sort of thing just happened by chance. I had a lot of big shrimp and started keeping them in a solid white bucket sunk down in the water overnight, and the shrimp went to the color of the bucket. They were solid white and just really lit up the water, just like a glow stick. And when you would cast them out, they were just great. They would change color to solid white. The snook loved them. They'd bite 'em. The snook'd bite them at the [Fort Pierce] Turning Basin at night. It was unbelievable.

Anyway, I cast out that morning. I always wanted a ten-pound or better trout. And I hooked this trout, and I had my friend from Kentucky fishing with me. When I hooked him, he came up. And I said, "Willie, if I get this one, this is going to be it, you know."

There were a lot of willow bushes at the time that hung over in the water, and that fish ran upstream, then he came back toward the bank, and he went under that willow. One of my tricks was to stick the rod as far down in the water as I could, and he came under there without getting hung and got it downstream of that willow. Then I got him up, and Willie netted him for me. It was the biggest trout at the time that was ever recorded there. I took it over to DeBrooks [Bait and Tackle Shop], and he recorded it at fourteen pounds.

I did write the story about it that came out in *Florida Sportsman*. I still have the story here somewhere, about the white shrimp and everything. I wrote it; they published it. It was a pretty good little story.

ELECTRICAL/LIGHTNING STORMS

I was in an electrical storm. The static in the air was just so strong your hair would stand up. I felt it through the steering wheel. You could feel it if you were standing in the water in the back of the boat. I've had lightning hit close enough to make the water turn red and boil. It's scary. And that thunderclap is right there, right as the lightning happens. Lightning is always one of my biggest fears being out there on the water. I figured out how to handle the wind and rain and about anything, but that lightning [laughs], that's a whole different ball game.

A BALE

One fellow I knew found a water-logged bale of marijuana. He took all the fish out of the fish box, put the bale down in the fish box, covered it all up with fish, and brought it home [laughs]. He was drying it out at his house in Fort Pierce, and when you turned off of U.S. 1 and went down toward his street, you started smelling it. You could smell it way before his street, it was that pungent. But that's about the only smuggling story I know. That's way in the past.

THE WARBIRD

I was fishing out on Northeast Grounds, circling. All of the kingfish boats were circling. Jack Albinson fished a yellow boat, a Lindsey, called the *Banana*. Jack and Wild Bill and I were docked right beside each other. I was fishing in tight circles. I looked over there at Jack, who was always dying or bleaching his curly hair. I saw one of those little warbirds. I don't understand why they call 'em warbirds. They're little bitty ones that get on your boat and fly around and end up dying. They say never let one die on your boat; it's bad luck.

That thing got on the top of Jack's head and got his feet tangled in his hair. He must have been in the middle of catching fish, so he brushed at it, and he couldn't get him out. Every time I'd come around, I'd see that bird [laughs] flopping around in his hair there. I'm laughing and got on the radio and told everybody about Jack and his damn bird. That was one of the funniest things I ever saw out there.

HITTING A TANKER

Jack Albinson was asleep and ran his boat into the side of a tanker. Jack was always terrible about sleeping in the morning. If he'd been a little bit further, the tanker would have run over him and probably killed him. He was on the autopilot. He'd gotten past the offshore bar, toward the shipping lanes. He was asleep and on the autopilot. On autopilot! I've done it myself. Pretty wild there; I would take naps while on autopilot.

My favorite, my very favorite, fishing, and not a whole lot of people do it, is grouper trolling. I got where I was pretty good at it. I'd dived the rocks and learned how they hide in the rocks and where they liked to go. I used my deck reel and put it way down on the bottom and had so much fun on that thing. Fishing right on the bottom, trolling about 4, 4½ knots, and when the big ones hit, it's like they're going to tear the reel right off the boat. It's just like having an orgasm [laughs].

Damn thing hit me, and I'd worry about getting them up to the top. I've caught 400 pounds in an hour doing that. Just as fast as I can go around, I'd catch another.

You troll about 4 knots. You can fish them just like you do kingfish. You use stainless steel wire you get at the welding shop here. It's .035, but it's real strong. You count so many turns down. One turn is three foot. But you have to adjust because everybody's reel is different. That's part of it, and learning how to fish the edges of the reefs and how to come in and out, where to fish, so if that fish gets on, it won't dive right under the rock and break off. You pull it across going away from the ledge when he hits.

The best way is to come straight across the edge, if you were fishing the 340 rock off of Fort Pierce, which was a really, really good grouper rock, and a really good kingfish rock, too. You would make a circle and come around, and when you see that edge, you sometimes count, like, one-thousand-one, one-thousand-two, one-thousand-three. That would help you figure the time when your bait came across down there, and he would hit it when you would be going away from the ledge. He wouldn't be able to dodge back underneath the ledge. Now, if he hits it on the front, he comes through the front part of the reef and under the reef, and he'd break off, and you'd lose him.

But I just loved that kind of grouper fishing. Tommy Jones liked it, too, but he's always said that I persevered at it. Sometimes I wouldn't get a bite for a couple hours, but I would still hang with it. Oh, I caught a lot of big kings down there, too. Lot of times, when we were fishing out here, in summer, you know, like about ten o'clock, you can't get a bite. Drop that thing down there and fish, you could adjust and fish any way you want to. You could tie a rag to mark it and drop it to a certain depth. I could use any depth I wanted to. But adjust it up and down and get where I'd catch a few, and that's where I would leave it.

A lot of days, especially in June, when the price is right for kingfish, you catch fifty to a hundred pounds extra when it's two-fifty a pound, and that's a big difference. Sometimes in the afternoon, if you stay late, they'll come back and bite shallow again, three or four o'clock. A lot of times, if you look at it when you're trolling, that bait will be close to the rocks down there. And the fish go down there and feed during the midday, and you'd catch 'em deep.

OVERBOARD ALONE

I was fishing 8A, which is one of the first spots where the kingfish land when they leave Daytona coming south. It's a reef and a great area to fish. I don't know why they call it 8A.

You can go across the shoals or you can go around them. The shoals rise up to six feet. So you go to a certain point off the Cape, going out of Cape Canaveral. You got to know to hit ninety degrees out till you get to a certain point, and then you have to turn sixty degrees, and you go right across the shoal at a certain number.

The shoals roll up there, and, if it's a ground swell, you don't cross it. You have to go all the way around it. But anyway, it's six feet. It's even shallower there in some places. A lot of boats hit the ground there. It's called Cape Shoals. The shoals are about six miles out. Once you cross the shoals, then it's about twelve miles out, about like it is here. And it's not a very big reef. Doesn't support a lot of boats, except when a lot of fish fall in all around it.

We'd been fishing every day, marathon fishing, catching our limits every day. It's rodeo fishing or marathon, whatever you want to call it. And I went out there tired. I'd been fishing every day. Just one trip a day. Most of us agreed to do that. It's not fair at all, to make more than one trip a day. Anyway, we'd catch fifty head of fish, or whatever the limit was at the time. But a lot of times you'd be through at nine o'clock in the morning.

That day it was cold, and I had on my slickers, and I had just bought a new pair of Croc fishing boots and—this is part of the story—they're real comfortable, and so I was proud of 'em. We're out there fishing. It wasn't that bad. It was a small ground swell that you would pop up over every once in a while. There was a little lull. And I was on the north end of probably thirty or thirty-five boats, and I was on the very north side of them in a circle catching fish. I sat down there on the back in the stern jerking the bug, and I was just restin' a little bit.[2]

Till this day, I'll never know why, but I turned to the side, and when I did, I took both feet off the bottom and popped up over one of them waves and did a flip. Went right over backwards, and when it happened, I thought, there's so many boats here, there's nothing to worry about; I'll be all right. It was a hard north tide, and my boat kept circling and going north. I was behind it, swimming, or trying to; in fact, a line came by me on my outrigger. My paravane came out, and I thought to grab it but then thought better. A king mackerel was on it, and it came right by me.

I was yelling, you know, "Help me, help me, help me, help me!" Everybody was catching fish, and those diesel motors were loud. I mean, I wasn't seventy-five feet from some of them, but they couldn't hear me.

I had all those rubbers and everything on, and I was sinking, and I had to try to get that off. So I got my rubber top off, and then I pulled my [laughs], I never will forget this, it was unbelievable, I pulled those Croc boots off. They were two black Croc boots, and I pulled them off. They came up and they stood straight up, just side by side each other, right on the top of the water, and started going away from me.

But I was having so much trouble, struggling to get this stuff off and stay afloat, that I was panicking. And that's the worst thing you can do when you're in the water is panic. So I calmed down enough to get my rubber pants off, but I still had on a sweatshirt, jeans, and socks. I was trying to get closer to the boats, but there was a north tide. I was pushed away from all the boats. My boat was a long, long ways further away from me.

I'd just gotten to the point where I said my prayers, and I knew what was going to happen next, because that's what happens when you drown. You just take a gulp of water and that's it. It fills your lungs and you go down.

I saw this boat. He was northwest of me, and I saw him circling and catching fish. That boat crossed about 100 to 150 feet from me. I was

---

2 A bug, also called a jig or a feather, is a hook with a feather attached that is used as a type of lure. They are often made by the fisherman or can be purchased in a fish house or tackle store.

yelling and screaming and screaming. Then I'd start sinking. Then I had to swim a little bit. And he never saw me, never saw me.

I knew I had one chance. I was in the water thirty minutes or more and was floundering. I couldn't get my sweatshirt off. When I tried to take it off, I'd sink too fast, and every time I tried to get it off I about drowned. Getting the other clothes off and not sinking was the hardest part. Once you get down to a certain depth, it's hard to get back to the surface.

I saw that boat circling there, and I saw him catch a fish, and I thought, he's coming back around. I was an avid swimmer when I was a young person, and I got on my back and backstroked as much as I could. I swam, and I thought this is my last try, and I knew I was gone. I swam and he came around. I yelled and yelled and yelled, and he finally saw me.

He cut the boat over, and I told him, "Grab hold of me. I can't stay up any longer." I was going. I'm pretty small, but they jerked me over into the boat. He and his son-in-law were fishing together. And I was in shock, then, too, but they saved me.

They were commercial fishermen out of Salerno. His name is Delton Nail. They called another boat and got his son-in-law off the boat. He got on the bow of the other boat and got behind my boat and nudged up to the back and eased up on the bow and jumped onto my boat and got it out of gear.

They said, "We'll take you in. We'll get him to drive your boat in."

And I said, "No, just give me a few minutes. Just put me back on my boat."

And he said, "By the way, you had three fish on when we stopped your boat."

When I was in the water a fish came right by me. That fish come right by my arm, and I was scared I was going to get caught by the hooks. I was trolling about 5 knots. With those big fish I always trolled faster. And I knew I couldn't pull myself all the way back to the boat. I was scared that hook was going to grab me and tow me, which would have drowned me. I was using wire leader. I always use wire. That was a pretty wild experience, trying to stay afloat.

Anyway, I got back on my boat, and I had thirty-some fish, and I went back fishing. I said, "If I don't go back now I might not ever go again in my life." One of my good friends, Mason Bowen, helped me catch the rest of my limit.

About two days later, it hit me like a sledgehammer how close I'd come, and then I didn't fish for about a week. But anyway, that was my near-drowning experience.

LOVE OF KINGFISHING

Well, I think I stayed at it. I just like the independence . . . the freedom. And I like to learn. I always loved the part about learning the ocean, learning the rocks, and just the challenge of tying my own rigs, tying my bugs, being able to fish the way I want to.

Hell, I'd go out there, and everybody'd come in. I'd just stay out there a lot of days, and I did well with it. Just ride the rocks and mostly troll for grouper out there. Everybody went in, but I'd stay, because the grouper price was so good. Catch a hundred pounds of them, and it'd be three-fifty, four hundred bucks.

Just learning the ocean and the rocks, the moon, and the tides, I still love all that. And every time I see a full moon I think about what's happening out in the ocean. Different things have happened, and I've always been amazed. Moby [Paul] taught me that the first day of a south tide, the grouper will bite. They come out from under the ridges, and they come up in the water. First day, and then the second day, you catch some, and then the third day, it's over with. But just learning stuff like that.

I'm going in the fall here, if I'm healthy enough. I always look forward to the first of November. I try to get everything ready. I get me a dock at the Cape Canaveral Marina. I head north. And then a lot of times we'll go up off of Daytona and fish that high ridge, that area up there, until those fish are pushed further south.

But the learning experience to me has been the most fun. And the independence of it.

THE FUTURE

So many boats have gotten into the fish, and they are mobile boats. They trailer them, and they can run anywhere. Mason Bowen and Ronney Skelley and me found those fish last winter, and I couldn't believe it. We found the fish on Pelican Flats. There were five or six boats there.

We unloaded that evening. The very next day out, there were fifty to seventy boats. And the next day, it was a hundred and some boats.

Three days. It was unbelievable. I mean, every kind of boats. You got dive boats, you got charter boats, everything that can get a license is out there. So the future doesn't look very good to me. But I'm hoping that things will change before y'all go.

I don't know what the National Marine Fisheries Service wants. I tell you, they don't want you. They want no commercial fishermen. They don't want you. Anything they can do to run you out, they'll do.

That's just like the grouper fishermen. You had to buy two permits to get one. Now they've taken everything where you can't catch but one of something. It's very hard to kingfish and grouper fish. You're either going to do one or the other to make any money. You can't do both like we used to do.

BROTHERHOOD

I must say one thing that I like a lot, and I appreciate a lot, is the friends and the comradeship. Just knowing the older fishermen, like Tommy Jones, Steve Lowe, Jimmy Turner, Willis Dugger, Flash [Charles] Bowen and his son, Mason, and hearing their stories and experiences is won-

Captain Jimmy Reeves bought and refitted A. J. Brown's boat, *Second Wind*. As a tribute to his friend, Jimmy had *A.J.* painted on the bow.

derful. In your mind, you say, "God, I'd like to do that" [laughs]. But, to me, that's meant a lot.

I just love the ocean. I love the part of being a mariner and being part of it all. I still love it. Whether I catch a fish or not, I still love it.

Coda

To be told that you only have six months to live is a terrifying prospect. A. J. Brown faced this ordeal with courage, calm, and dignity, although his good friend Tommy Jones did affectionately observe that he looked "pretty pitiful" during his final hours in the Hospice center in Fort Pierce.

A. J. Brown died on December 24, 2009. Fishermen from all over Florida came to his funeral to honor one of the greatest and most respected kingfish captains of his time.

Due to the long and odd hours, marriages and relationships with fishermen can be difficult. That was not so with A. J. Brown and his love for the last ten years of his life, artist Sherry Horton. They were both solitary people and got along handsomely. A. J. was fortunate to have Sherry by his side until the end.

A. J. Brown and his love, artist Sherry Horton.

3

Captain Ray Perez

University student, revolutionary, counterrevolutionary, and refugee are terms that describe the amazing life of Captain Ray Perez. But he always has been and continues to be a fisherman.

He was born in Cojimar, Cuba, the fishing village that was frequented by Ernest Hemingway and provided the setting for the novel *The Old Man and the Sea*. As a teenager Ray auditioned for the role of Manolin, the young boy in the story, but was considered too old for the part. In his own Hemingway-esque moment, however, Ray did once catch a 750-pound marlin by hand while fishing in a small skiff off Cojimar.

While he was a student at the Institute of Havana, Ray joined Castro's Revolution to overthrow the brutal dictator, Fulgencio Batista. After the Revolution, Ray became disillusioned with the communists and Castro's unrestrained use of firing squads. He escaped in the night from Cuba to Florida in his small 21-foot fishing boat, loaded with nineteen other refugees.

He then found work as a shark fisherman in Fort Pierce, Florida. Don Clark (Ray's friend who drew the illustration of Ray's *Grand Cru*) said that in the 1960s he used to see Ray and Chief Anselmo Santes entering the inlet loaded down with sharks. He said their boat would shake because it was so full of large, live sharks lashed and tied all over it.

Captain Ray Perez has participated in many kinds of commercial fishing and is still one of the east coast's finest hand-line commercial kingfish captains. He lives on a five-acre tropical estate in western Fort Pierce. His father and former fishing partner also has a house on the property, where they raise chickens, tropical fruits, and vegetables. A full mechanical shop, a gym (to keep in shape when he is not fishing), a swimming pool, and several sheds and chicken coops can be found on Ray's estate. Our interviews were always cut short in the early

Ray and wife Bobbie, his fishing partner.

afternoons when Ray and his wife and everyone at the estate would retire for their regular afternoon siesta.

Today Captain Perez fishes almost every day with his wife and fishing partner, Bobbie. Together they nearly always produce healthy catches. When other boats don't fish because of the bad weather or ocean conditions, they'll fish. When it's too rough in the ocean, they'll troll or jig for jacks, bluefish, and pompano in the Indian River Lagoon. Even in strong westerly winds the Perezes fish along the beach. By going every day, they catch enough to have the bigger fish checks at the end of the week. Captain Perez believes that the best way to catch the most fish is to fish the most. And that is what he does.

Ray Perez in His Own Words

I was born on May 7, 1941, in the little town of Cojimar, which is east of Havana. That's where all the rafters organized and left from when the rafts came to Florida in the late 1980s.[1]

My father worked for the railroad in Cuba and he also fished—he was a commercial fisherman, too. He fished for swordfish and marlins mostly. He fished similar to the longlines used by swordfish boats today,[2] only theirs was a shorter version. They had one big square float with three floats floating off of that one, with a drop out of each one of them. They would drop a leader coming off from the buoys at depths down from twenty to a hundred fathoms. There were three hooks at each drop. They had three hooks every square and about the same at each drop. Where there was three buoys, each had three hooks on it. He had an 18-foot kind of homemade boat. He had a little—I think it was an 18-horse—Palmer inboard engine. From our hometown to the Florida Straits is about a mile from the beach. It was deep enough water to catch swordfish and marlins.

THE OLD MAN AND THE SEA

The movie was made in my town. I almost went into movie acting because I could speak English, and at the time that they were making the movie, they couldn't find anybody else. But I was too old to play the part of the boy, so that kind of put me off of it. I think I was thirteen, fourteen, or something like that. They wanted a much younger boy to be with the old man.

I met the actors. I met Hemingway, too. He'd show up every once in a while when they were making the movie. He used to come to Cojimar quite a bit. He liked the little town. He'd come to eat and drink. I met the actor Spencer Tracy there, too. He never said much; he was kind of

---

1 Many empty Cuban rafts drifted up the Gulf Stream past Fort Pierce and, because of their steel frames, were serious navigational hazards, especially in the dark.

2 Longline fishing is a commercial fishing technique. It uses a longline, called the "main line," with baited hooks attached at intervals by means of branch lines called "snoods." A snood is a short length of line attached to the main line using a clip or a swivel with the hook at the other end. Longlines are classified mainly by where they are placed in the water column—at the surface or at the bottom. Lines can also be set by means of an anchor or left to drift. Hundreds or even thousands of baited hooks can hang from a single line. Longliners commonly target swordfish, tuna, halibut, sablefish, and many other species.

a quiet guy. I wasn't that close with Hemingway. I just met him a time or two. Most of it was filmed in Cojimar, which means "I went to the sea" or "I found the sea."

THE REVOLUTION

I joined with Castro because the government then was run by Batista. It was a dictatorship. There were too many bad things happening. There was too much abuse against the people. That's what created the Revolution. Batista was abusive to the people, to the ones that didn't agree with him. You know how a dictatorship is: if they didn't like what you did or said, they'd just kill you. I mean, back there, there's no judge or jury or trial. He took the government by power, by military coup. Under Batista there were dead bodies all over the damn place.

I was a student at the Institute of Havana getting my bachelor's degree. I was in college for three years and studying science and letters. I was planning on studying medicine. You had to have both science and letters to get into medicine. I had two more years to go to get my bachelor's degree and then go to the university to get my medical degree.

There was a multitude of students that joined the Revolution. All the young people were against the government. They just got connected through the underground. Oh, it was dangerous. We went into the mountains with Castro's people to train. But you really just trained as you went. Mostly, you just gained experience in the field, and most people got their own guns somehow. They had them or got them in the fights and in the battles. That was the Revolution.

Before I went with Castro to the mountains, I was fighting in the underground in Havana. We would be planning attacks on police stations, and in 1957, we went to the Palace House where the president lived.

ATTACK ON THE PRESIDENTIAL PALACE

About a half a dozen of us got out of there alive; the rest of them all died in there. Probably about twenty or thirty of us went into the President's Palace just fighting and shooting. The palace guards weren't prepared for us. We had Brazilian hand grenades that didn't work. They were a failure, but we didn't find out until we were in there. We commandeered a bus and used that bus to ride right by the Palace House, dropped out right at the front door, and proceeded to go in. I got to the second floor and had to turn back. The grenades weren't working, and we were just getting demolished by their force. They had better weapons than we did, and it was just a bad day. It was just another day in the Revolution.

I'd been in some close calls during the Revolution. The same day, I was running around and heard shots. I felt stuff all over my head that was sticking, and I was scratching my head. I'd been shot at, and it was just the plaster of the column. I thought I was behind the column, but I was on the wrong side [laughs]. They cut my hair with a machine gun bullet. That was a little too close for comfort. That was when I came back outside of the palace. To get away, I just ran around buildings and through alleys. They didn't chase too far, because we were still shooting back. Six of us made it out.

The Revolution was really not good. I lost a lot of young friends. I don't really . . . much want to talk about it. When Castro came down out of the mountains, it was over. Batista had left before that and went to Spain.

DISILLUSIONED

After Castro took power, it wasn't long before we were disillusioned, especially after he killed his best friend, Camilo. Camilo had a lot of followers, and Fidel got scared that Camilo was going to take power away from him—not kill him, but just take the people away from Castro. Camilo was just a friend of Castro's. He was one of the first ones that went down there on the *Gramma*, the boat that took Castro from Mexico to the mountains of Cuba.

I was more close to Castro than to Camilo. Castro knew me, and I knew him well, or thought I did. Castro was just a leader. I mean, every force has got to have a leader, a commander. I knew Che very little.

Like I said, Castro had betrayed us, because he always denied being communist. He was always going to have elections and a democratic government, and then he just turned that all around. It was going to be a democratic government after the Revolution. Most of the people were with him in the beginning. Then they all left him. He gained a lot of other people after the Revolution was won. After he came down from the mountains, a lot of people joined him. It was easy then to be a revolutionary [laughs]. And those people that never did anything during the Revolution are the people that stayed with him. The ones that did most of the fighting all left.

When I first came to this country, I had already been fighting in the counterrevolution against him, and I was running with a friend of mine. They were close on our tail, and I told him, "Listen, I'm leaving. You better get your ass and go with me because they're going to get you." I'd been here about a month, and I learned that they got him and executed him. They just got him and put him to the wall. His name was René.

The Revolution was in 1959. I came to the United States in 1961. We replaced one dictator with a worse one. We got out of the frying pan into the fire.

CROSSING THE STRAITS

We fished for swordfish and marlin mostly. My father fished, and my grandfathers from both sides of the family were both fishermen. My mama's family was all fishermen. Most of them are dead. Most of the others all came to the United States in the early '60s.

I was nineteen when I came over on the same boat I was fishing. We planned it for about a week or so. We loaded up a bunch of people on it and took off. We just went fishing one night and kept going. We just decided we're going. We left because the communists were getting too bad.

I had a 21-foot fishing boat at the time with a little 2-cylinder Palmer engine. I think it was 45 horses or something like that. It took me fourteen or fifteen hours to get from Havana to Big Pine Key, where we landed. We had eighteen people in it. It was stacked, and it was blowing a northwester about 25, 30 miles an hour. We always kept a canvas on the boat for bad weather, so we put everybody under the canvas and pulled it all the way back and snapped it down. You see, it was an open boat with a bow cap on it. There was one opening, back by the tiller. We just pulled the canvas around, and the water would just wash over.

One of the passengers was my girlfriend, Nancy, and her sister. Nancy later became the mother of my daughter, America. Nancy wasn't my wife then; she was just a friend. Out of the eighteen people, I only knew three. The rest of them were unknown. They knew my fishing partner, and arrangements were worked through connections. They paid my uncle, and my uncle distributed money to my family, because when I left, my father and mother and my brother were still there.

With that load [on the boat] and in that wind, it did maybe 5 knots. It was against a northwest wind, blowing against the Gulf Stream current. It wasn't so bad down there because the Gulf Stream is running straight east until it gets through the Straits, and then it turns or starts turning to the north. So the northwest wind is usually not that bad. That day was bad, because it was blowing 25 miles an hour. It was a March cold front.

As a matter of fact, it was March 13, the same day as the attack on the President's Palace in 1957. This was March 13, 1961. I never liked the month of March too good.

THE UNITED STATES

The Sheriff's Department of Monroe County, I guess, in Key West and immigration authorities down there treated us okay. They took us to Key West and put us in a hotel overnight. Next day, they brought us to Miami, and we went through like a trial in front of a judge, and we were granted political asylum. This was in 1961. I was paroled in this country for an indefinite time on political asylum. They couldn't deport us back to Cuba, no matter what they did, as long as Castro was there. It was political asylum.

MARIEL

In 1980 I went down to Mariel to get my family and took Herman Summerlin's boat, *Easy Money*. They had already changed the name from *Sea Lady II* to the *Easy Money*. I didn't bring anybody back 'cause when I got to Mariel, I found out that all the people, my daddy and my mama and my son, were already in Key West.

Oh, that was another thing. I had a son down there that was nineteen years old. He was born nine months to the day after I left Cuba. I didn't know his mama was pregnant. He's three months older than my daughter, America. But he's from another mother. Couldn't be the same mother; they're three months apart [laughs].

Easy Money was a 55-foot boat with a 1292 turbo diesel motor. I had Uncle Bill Summerlin and Denny Moore with me on that trip. We went to Mariel, and we spent about fourteen days there. I had a list of the people that I wanted to bring back with my family and Larry Masters.

Larry is Howard Masters's son and was in jail in Cuba because he landed a plane down there for some unknown reason. While I was down there, I met a friend of mine from the Revolution, and he told me, "Ray, I got all those people out of here. You don't have to." But he said, "I can't get Larry out. Larry's a political prisoner. The United States has to deal with him."

Since he got everybody else out, I left. When he told me that, I trusted the man. We had fought together in the Revolution. When he was saying he got everybody out, my mom and dad and son were already in Key West. So all I had left down there was my brother and his family. And when this guy told me that they already were shutting the port down, and the United States was already closing it up, I just left about a week later. My brother was here, and all the people I had on my list were already out.

Many people helped out with the fuel and groceries and stuff and contributed enough to make it possible for me to go down there and get my family. They gave me names on the list besides my family. It was in 1980, and I spent my birthday there in Mariel, Cuba.

There were so many boats there, you could hardly move around in that damn port, and that's a big port. We just anchored out. I think the rafts were ten years later. The Mariel Boatlift was in '80, and the raft, I think, it was mostly in the '90s.

HOUSE OF TWENTY-ONE

It's funny, because I came here to replace a Negro. There was a sign at the refugee center in Miami that they needed some shark fishermen here in Fort Pierce. Dave Putnam and Dan Horton had a shark-fishing operation in Fort Pierce, and they needed some fishermen for the boats. They knew the Cubans had been in the shark-fishing business for years, so they put a sign on the refugee center down there, asking for some shark fishermen.

I was living in this big house in Miami at the time. They called it the House of Twenty-One, because there was twenty-one of us living there. There were a handful of us playing blackjack when Don Horton came in to pick up the Cubans who had signed up for the job at the refugee center. But one of them was black, and in '61 a black person wasn't allowed anywhere near the docks here. In the early '60s, they had their own bathroom and their own drinking fountains, and they weren't allowed out after dark on the streets, and he was a black Cuban fisherman. There were a half a dozen that came, and the black guy couldn't even live in the same hotel with the rest of them. God, they had to put him somewhere else.

They decided he better stay down there in Miami. And I said, "Hell, I'll go. I got nothing else better to do."

Twenty-one people lived in the house, and blackjack is twenty-one. It was just a coincidence.

I left Nancy in Miami when I first came to Fort Pierce. I wanted to see what happened first. I wasn't going to stay; I was going to go back to Miami. While up there, I stabbed myself—I still got the little mark there—skinning a shark. I went back to Miami and then a short time later had to go back to Fort Pierce to get some stitches taken out.

I said, "Okay, I might as well go back, and I'm going to stay." I loaded them up, and Nancy and I came and stayed here. That was July 3, 1961, and I've been here since.

SHARK FISHING

I was fishing sharks here in Fort Pierce with Chief Anselmo Santes. We were fishing for Dan Horton and Dave Putnam, who owned the boat. They had several boats, and we were fishing one of them.

That's how Shark Island got the name, because that's where we processed the sharks. We brought them in, skinned them, dried the skins out, and dried the fins. We dumped the meat overboard right there. We had a big dock, and the dock was about forty-foot long and about twenty-foot wide. There was a little house on the island, too. It was probably about twenty by forty. Since then the island has shrunk. The dock was bigger than the island is now. The island was a lot bigger then. The island was probably at least a hundred by a hundred. It had a lot of trees on it.

There were two little islands. They've always been separated, and there's a slough right between those two little islands, real deep, because we used to go through there with a shrimp boat. I went there when I was jack fishing in the Indian River Lagoon. That hole is still pretty deep.

In the house we had two long tables. That's where we'd sit after we skinned the sharks. We'd work on that plywood and put salt on them and cure them before we shipped them to New Jersey.

We were just selling the hides and the fins. At first they were saving the liver oil, but they couldn't sell it. By the time we started, they came out with the synthetic vitamins, and the livers became worthless. They didn't want the oil anymore.

CATCHING SHARKS

We had 3,000 feet of cable with about 300 hooks. That cable'd go right to the bottom with an anchor and a float on each end. This was not like a swordfishing line. It was not a drifting line. It was set on the bottom. We caught all kinds of sharks. We caught duskies and hammerheads and a lot of tigers. Big-ass tigers back then.

Sharks were plentiful. Big cash. We were catching fifteen, twenty, thirty sharks a day. We were generally fast. It didn't take us long to dress out and skin the sharks. To keep the knives sharp we had a wet rock and had a steel in one hand and the knife in the other. We were sharpening the whole time, because shark hide will eat the edge of a knife in a heartbeat. Depending on the size of the shark, it'd take about a minute a foot to dress and skin it. Probably, fourteen- or fifteen-footers were about the biggest.

We fished for Don Horton and Dave Putnam for a year or two, and then we went back to work but still fished at nights and weekends. Chief went to work for John Deere, and I went to work for Mosquito Control in St. Lucie County. Then I went to work for Bob Drum at Law's Boat Yard in Fort Pierce. It was where Harbortown Marina is today, at the mouth of Taylor Creek. There used to be an old railway to pull the boats out on. At the time, all the old fish houses were down there on Taylor Creek—Parker's, D&D, and Seven Seas.

Chief was working for Herman Summerlin at the Seven Seas Fish House. I had subcontracted with Sears and was doing chain link fence installation, shingle roofing, and aluminum carports and siding.

A guy that was working for me in the chain link fence business had an old boat in his yard and gave it to me. Chief and I fixed it up, and we started shark fishing with that little boat. We were fishing 3,000 feet of cable on that thing with 300 hooks. It was a 20-foot boat and had a 6-cylinder Willis [Jeep engine]. Chief and I took it out of a car, took the radiator off of it, put a saltwater pump on it, and cooled it with saltwater, raw water. We used the transmission and clutch, and we fished with that. We made enough money with that little boat to buy a 40-footer and kept fishing with that.

Ray Perez (*left*), fishery biologist Dale S. Beaumariage (*center*), and Anselmo Santes ("Chief") shark fishing off Fort Pierce in the 1960s.

Ray sharpening the skinning knife.

After a while, we had a problem with Ocean Leathers, the company in New Jersey that bought the hides. They were downgrading our hides all the time and trying to pay us less money. So I got on the truck one time with a shipment of hides and went up there. And on that trip most

Ray and Chief skinning sharks.

of the hides were graded real good. But I couldn't go to New Jersey every time we had a shipment, and after that we just quit shark fishing.

Chief's full name is Anselmo Santes. He was a part-time fisherman in Cuba and also worked at a tobacco warehouse where they stored big bales of tobacco. He favored Batista during the Revolution. I didn't want to talk about it [the Revolution] with him.

SHARK BAIT

We started on our own with a little 20-footer and were fishing 3,000 feet of cable, 300 hooks that lay on the bottom. Back then, the fishermen used to save the bonitos and the jacks and all the trash fish for us to use for bait, and broken up mackerel from the nets. Every once in a while, when the bait was scarce, we'd just harpoon a porpoise. They come running in front of the boat. We used a lily iron. It's a little like an arrow with an arrowhead. On the back of it there's a hole for a shaft fixer, and the middle of that thing has a hole where you put a cable through. When you harpoon it, it goes in and when you pull the harpoon out and you pull on your line, the lily iron gets crossways in the dolphin [porpoise], and it stays there.

Then we just brought them in close to the boat, and we didn't have nothing back then but a little .22 rifle or a baseball bat. That's what we used mostly, a baseball bat. We used it for sharks or porpoise. The harpoon hurt 'em pretty badly. I tried to put the harpoon right beside the dorsal fin, and that gets the lungs and everything else on them and just about kills them.

When they were dead, we'd just lay them across the bow of the boat and open them up from the back and cut the meat chunks out of it. They were about one-pound chunks. We'd take the shark line out, and we'd set it, leave it, and go pick it up the next day. We'd fish anywhere from two miles offshore of Pepper Park to the Northeast Grounds. We also fished 12 Buoy, 12A Buoy, and around the offshore bar, inshore bar, and all over the place. We'd look for good bottom, then we'd set it close to the edge of the rocks and try to set on the sand so they don't get tangled up. Every once in a while we'd set it on the rocks, and we'd get a hellacious jewfish [goliath grouper] on those things.

Most of the time, we'd lay the sharks across the bow of the boat and skin them. Threw the carcass back overboard and just folded up the hides. All we brought in was the hides and the fins. The rest of it we just threw back overboard. When we fished the big boat, the *Miss Carmen*, we brought them into Shark Island and cleaned them there. We couldn't load the big ones and had to drag them in. Then we'd pull them up on the dock and skin them out at Herman's at Baywood Fish House.

BIG TIGER SHARK

We caught one big tiger shark that had two turtles inside of him. I don't know how big, but he was big. The two turtles inside of him were at least two feet across. I think Herman still has the jaws from that shark. The turtles were hanging on the wall of Astor's Baywood fish house.

We'd have as many as thirty-some sharks' hides on that boat. We often had maybe eight or ten big ones hanging on the side, because we couldn't load them up. Sometimes we had that little boat loaded pretty heavy, because we had the hides and stuff down on the deck and still had some big sharks hanging on the sides. Some of them we'd load up

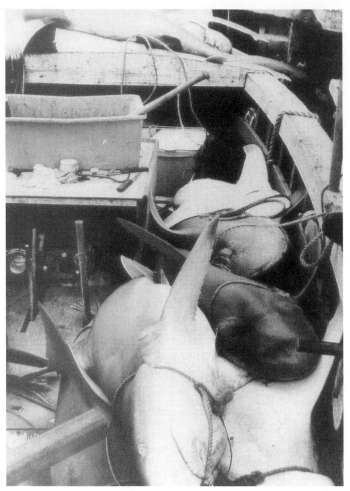

Ray and Chief's boat had a Willis Jeep engine. They steered from a tiller in the stern. The gearshift and throttle can be seen behind the engine box. Note the baseball bat, their weapon for dispatching the sharks. Longtime Fort Pierce resident Don Clark said their boat used to vibrate and shake as they came in the inlet because of the sharks on it and lashed to it.

over the stern and on the pile cab. It'd take us five hours to come from north of 12A Buoy, about three miles out from the inlet, dragging them damned sharks.

With the little boat with the little 6-cylinder Willis, we made enough money to buy an old 40-foot wooden sports boat and made it into a shark boat. But when we took it out in the ocean and started beating around, the damn screws would fall out of it. I'd jump overboard and

Salted shark skins. Note the bag of Morton Salt.

Salted shark fins taken from processed sharks.

drive pegs back in the holes. We had the damn line out and were hauling the line, and sharks were all over the damn place. Chief tied a line
around my waist, and if he'd see a shark coming, he'd just pull me out.
I'd put them pegs in where the nails fell out to keep from sinking. We
had three or four bilge pumps on the damn thing, running all the time.

Baywood Fish House in the 1960s, South Beach Causeway, Fort Pierce. A public beach and boat ramp is located there today.

This was an old sports boat and was a nice-looking boat. For power, we had two big Chrysler Royals, I think they were, with twin down-draft carburetors. That thing would suck gas like mad. I mean it's a good thing gas was cheap back then.

KINGFISHING

Back then, mackerel fishing was in full swing. Chief got a little boat, and I got a little boat, and that's when we started kingfishing and bottom fishing. There was a lot of snapper and grouper and kingfish, too. It was nothing to go out there in the morning and catch 2,000 pounds of kingfish before noon. This was in the late '60s, early '70s.

There was a big fleet. This fleet out here now ain't nothing compared to what it used to be back then. We went snapper- or bottom-fishing when there was no kingfish or kingfish were slow. Sometimes the fish houses didn't want them because we got too damn many, and we got

Loading a large shark onto the dock at Baywood fish house. *Left to right:* unknown; shark researcher, Dale S. Beaumariage (with glasses); Ray Perez (with cigarette); Tom Maloney; and Archie Summerlin (bending forward).

shut off. Then I went bottom-fishing, and I went net fishing a couple of times, just to help out, but I never cared that much for net fishing—too much work.

Today, there's not the amount of kingfish that there used to be. I think the drift nets had a lot to do with it. And the airplanes and circle nets. The net fishing about ruined kingfishing.

THE START OF COMMERCIAL SWORDFISHING IN FLORIDA

I was the one that started longline swordfishing. I knew there had to be swordfish here, because I fished for them in Cuba, and I knew they

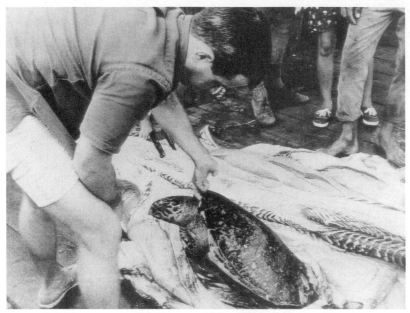

Tom Maloney inspects a perfectly preserved hawksbill turtle taken from the stomach of the Baywood shark. Because of the turtle's pristine condition, Beaumariage believes the shark swallowed the turtle whole and then almost immediately took the baited fishermen's hook.

harpooned them up to the north. I knew they had to come through the Florida Straits and up the Gulf Stream, because they're migratory fish. We caught swordfish in Cojimar. It's the first little port east of Havana.

When we started here, I just put together scrap and crab-trap buoys and stuff like that. I put together about a mile of line and had about thirty hooks. Denny McGauran went with me. It had to be in the '70s. We'd set the line with one pole and ball on it and tied it up to the boat. The rest of them were crappy buoys.

I turned loose of it to check the line with a spotlight. I was about 150 fathoms when I started checking it and saw a buoy going down. Then I'd go to the next buoy, and that one was going down, too. That was the last I saw of it. The whole line went.

On that particular trip I had mullet for bait, one mullet on each hook. Just put the hooks through the tail, bring it out to the side of the mullet head, hook it through the head, and tie it to the small leader cable. The buoys were supposed to hold the line up in the water.

After that trip, Ronnie Baird caught a swordfish while tilefishing.

Fort Pierce native and owner of the Baywood Fish house Herman Summerlin with shark.

And he asked me how to rig the line. When I told him how to rig the line, he went back out and started catching swordfish. He was the first one after me, and then everybody else went out and started swordfishing.

I was reading that part of your first book [*Great Kingfish Captains*] where Steve Lowe started going out and on that one trip caught all the fish. Like Tommie Jones says, "Steve, you're just a lucky man." He was going offshore with his gear when he found out there was another boat offshore. He set back the other way and caught all those fish. If he would have kept going the way he was headed, he wouldn't have caught crap. I was on the boat with him on that trip. My daughter Delores longlined with me, too.

Ray and his kingfish boat at his home in Fort Pierce. On the day this picture was taken, he was repairing damage done when he drifted up on the beach in Jupiter in 2010.

BAD WEATHER

There's been a lot of nasty weather out there longlining. I had 'em when they're blowing 70 miles an hour, blowing over the top of the radar dome on the *Grand Cru*. That was northeast of the Bahamas. My dad and I were swordfishing, and we just laid to. Dad and I fished that boat for about four years. We just drifted in that 75-mile-per-hour blow.

When you lay to, you just lay along sideways to the wind. Sometimes the waves would break over the top of it every once in a while, but the boat has a real low profile, and all the weight was down below. The ice hole and the engine weight was low. It was a Whitaker that Herman Summerlin salvaged. They build them down in Stuart, Florida.

LIGHTNING

I don't think I ever been hit by lightning, but it hit close enough to me one time that it picked me off the damn deck about a foot [laughs]. It hit that close to the boat. I mean, it just picked me up. I don't know how close it was. All I saw was just a flash and the noise and the jumping.

Ray and swordfish on the *Grand Cru*.

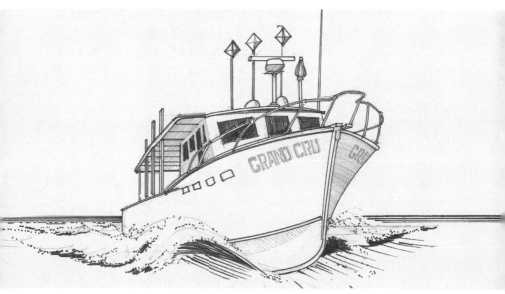

Captain Ray Perez's boat, *Grand Cru*. (Drawing by Don Clark.)

WATERSPOUTS

You don't want to get caught in a waterspout. I've seen 'em. I've been a hundred feet from them, but I've never been hit by one.

BIG MARLIN IN CUBA

I caught tunas over a thousand pounds. I also caught marlins over a thousand pounds. I caught a nice one in Cuba. Biggest marlin I caught in Cuba was over 700 pounds. All by hand. We just wore it out. It took us four hours to get it to the boat. We were following the fish, letting line out and taking line in; put some buoys on it and let him drag some buoys, too, while you're working with him. You just tire it down, just wear it out. It couldn't run too fast pulling the boat. At least you were lined up to it when it was running. It wasn't dragging the boat sideways. You had a little help going after him. It was back and forth. He'd drag us a little, and then we'd drag it back a little bit. You gaff it, bring it close to the boat, and then you just hit it on the head with a club. You got to grab the bill and pull the head up and just whack it on the head with a club. Then we got it in it.

It was that same 21-foot boat we came to Florida in. We had to load it over the stern so it wouldn't flip the boat. The head was all the way to the bow of the boat, and the tail was sticking out a few feet behind the boat. When we got to it, we took it off the other main line and had a coil of line on the boat to work the fish, took the leader off the main line, and tied it up to the line we were working with. Then work the fish in and out and put buoys on him to add some resistance. It was cotton line. I don't remember the strength.

The 800-pound tuna we caught in Florida was probably a thousand-pound fish with the head and the tail and the guts in it. The leader was only 400-pound test. But the longline was just like a rubber band.

In Cuba we had other fishermen around us, and they came onto our boat and helped us get the big marlin on board. My fishing partner and me couldn't have loaded that big fish by ourselves.

BIGGER FISH IN FLORIDA

While swordfishing, I caught marlins and tunas bigger than that one, but I had to release them; you couldn't keep them. At the time when I caught that tuna, all you could keep was one tuna. And sometimes we

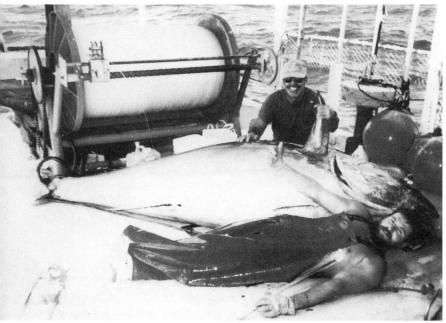

Ray's boat, the *Grand Cru,* rigged for swordfishing. Ray's crew—Robert Wasner and a huge tuna.

catch six on a day. The same thing with marlin: we had to release them all. And most of them were dead, same with the tuna. By the time we got him to the boat, it was dead.

My biggest catches of kingfish were in the late '60s, early '70s. I had a little teak Chris Craft, and then I had a 26-footer homemade built by Ray Lowe. Jerry Stohl used to fish it.

EMPTY BOATS

I'd seen some empty boats floating out here. One of them looked like it could have been either a Cuban or a Bahamian boat. It was probably 18 or 20 feet. It was just a homemade wooden island-type boat just floating full of water.

MISSILES

I remember, one night, it had to be a submarine shooting missiles. I seen this shit going out of the water [laughs]. It was out there northeast of the Bahamas. It was just like rockets coming out of the water. You know how they fire a rocket, all the fire coming out, just coming out of the water. I figured it just had to be a submarine. I don't believe in that other stuff.

I was just laying out there, waiting for morning to pick up my line. I saw one, and then a little while later, the other one coming out of the water. They could have been five miles or twenty miles away, but they were far away, because I didn't hear noise. I just saw them. It had to be a submarine, because I know there were submarines out there all the damn time.

HUMOROUS STORIES

The night the flying fish hit Chief in the mouth, he was smoking a cigar, and we're going out there when the flying fish hit him right square in the cigar. He must'a thought that the devil had his ass.

Then another time Jimmy Leal was sleeping on the boat. We were bottom-fishing at night, and he was laying down to sleep when a damned seagull crawled down in the cabin with him and landed on his head. It landed on his head! Yeah, and he came out of that cabin like the devil had him, too.

PORPOISE

My opinion about the porpoise is they're worse than titties on a boar hog. They ain't worth nothing. All they do is eat their weight in fish every twenty-four hours, and they don't do nothing for nothing. That's all they're good for. They always take your fish. When the fishermen aren't out there, they're forced to do their own. But they're just like thieves.

Those porpoise, they patrol that offshore bar, go up to Bethel Shoals, and then they come back. You see them running back and forth there. And if you get to a piece of rock that you know, and there's some fish there, you might catch a few before the porpoise get to you. And when they get there, you might as well pick it up and go, because you ain't going to catch shit.

FUTURE

I think that something good could be done for the fish out here yet, because there's still so much fish in Louisiana and Texas and the Gulf Coast. Why not in here? They came back to the Gulf Coast, because they have more fish coming from the west side of the Gulf. Fishing's still good up in Sebastian. You can go to Daytona, and fishing is still good. You could go south and still find good fishing.

It's just this area here because of the porpoise, and not only the porpoise. You don't see the bait here anymore. I do a lot of bottom-fishing at night in the summertime here, and there's no bait. The tides have been all screwed up, and the water's been cold. Something's wrong. It could just be a cycle.

FORT PIERCE ESTATE

I bought this five-acre and a quarter section about fifteen years ago. I have chickens and rabbits and all kinds of fruit trees. I've got avocados and mangos, almonds, and we've got a zapote tree. Bananas, passion fruit, an Annona tree, a starfruit tree, and coconut trees. I've got figs,

Ray in his shop on his estate in western Fort Pierce.

guavas, lemons, and limes. I had a lot of oranges and grapefruit, but the hurricanes just destroyed 'em. There are some oranges left, but they just never did well since Hurricanes Frances, Jeanne, Charley, and Wilma.

BORN FISHERMAN

I was born a fisherman. Since a little kid, I was born and raised right by the water. And my family were all fishermen. It's in the blood, I guess. I never could stay very long at a job. I always went back fishing. I worked for Mosquito Control two or three years. I had it damn good, and, well, I had a good deal with Sears, too. But I had to go back fishing. The same when I worked at Mosquito Control. I had a lot of freedom with Mosquito Control, because I was outside all the time.

But even when I was little in Cuba, between school and stuff, I was always fishing.

Anymore though, it's just too much government, and too damn many porpoises out there. And I don't feel like traveling anymore, like I done before. You know, like going to Louisiana or going out there to the Carolinas and all.

I do like fishing. I still like commercial fishing; I just don't enjoy it as much as I used to anymore, because—the same with the longlining—there's just too much government regulation, beside the fact that nobody wants to work. That's one of the reasons I sold that big boat, because I couldn't get a crew no matter how much you paid them. They make two or three thousand dollars and then you couldn't find them to go on another trip until they ran out of money. But I'll never give it up. Fishing's in my blood.

4

Captain Glenn Cameron

There is something fine and glorious about gliding over the clear blue sea at 40 to 50 miles per hour at the controls on a flying bridge nearly two stories above the ocean, with 1,600 diesel horsepower purring quietly three decks below. The great charter boats of today are true chariots of the gods, and those who captain them are kings.

Captain Glenn Cameron is the youngest captain interviewed for this book and the only native Floridian. Like many of Florida's commercial and charter captains, he grew up surfing and fishing off Florida's beaches. Glenn fished on the ocean with his father and brothers. He mated for some of the most renowned charter captains on Florida's east coast and earned his own captain's license at an early age.

Today, Glenn Cameron is easily one of the best charter tuna- and billfishing captains in Florida or anywhere. He has won all of the major billfish tournaments on the east coast of Florida and in the Bahamas at least once and has won some of them numerous times. He has fished all over the world.

When the rich and the powerful want to fish the ocean, they seek the very best captains available to guide them. Because of his vast experience and amazing skill as a charter captain, Glenn Cameron is in worldwide demand. He spends much of the year fishing in Mexico, the Bahamas, and Venezuela and is generally booked solid. His is truly a magical existence.

Since I first interviewed Glenn in 2009, he has turned his boat, *Floridian*, over to Captain Kevin Paul, his former mate, and is taking over as captain of the 58-foot *Zeus*. It is a Dean Johnson–built boat owned by Captain Sandy Smith, a former competitor and director of the Southern Kingfish Association (SKA).

Smith has been a major SKA contender. As *Fort Pierce Tribune*

Captain Glenn Cameron.

Zeus entering the Fort Pierce City Marina.

Kevin Paul (KP) and Captain Glenn conversing on the bridge of second *Floridian*.

outdoor editor Ed Killer put it, "Smith came in second on the SKA pro tour three times including once by .08 ounces! That's the best seven of ten fish in five states over eight months, and he was in second by the weight of an ice cube, or a finger flick of slime off a Kingfish. Sandy Smith was one of the most intense competitors in the history of the Southern Kingfish Association."

Together, Glenn Cameron and Sandy Smith are a fearsome fishing duo and are on a holy quest to win all of the major billfishing tournaments in the western Atlantic and Caribbean. In the 2010–2011 east coast billfish season, *Zeus* racked up impressive victories in major tournaments, winning the New Smyrna Beach Billfish Invitational, Finest Kind Quickie Invitational Sailfish Tournament, Bacardi Rum Billfish Tournament, Central Abaco Championship, and the Harbor Island Championship. Add to that their second-place showings in the Cape Eleuthera Championship and the Treasure Cay Championship, and you see why, as a team, Glenn Cameron and Sandy Smith are to big-time ocean tournament billfishing what Derek Jeter and Alex Rodríguez are to Major League Baseball.

Glenn Cameron in His Own Words

I was born October 29, 1963, in Melbourne, Florida. I'll be forty-seven here in a little bit. I'm one of the younger captains. That's scary. Actually, I grew up in the Palm Bay, Sebastian, Micco area. My dad was a contractor, developer.

We always owned fishing boats the whole time I was growing up. We started with a 26-foot Malibu that we completely gutted and had to rebuild before we were allowed to go fishing on it. From there, we bought another piece-of-junk boat that we fixed up, and so on and so forth. We just kept getting gradually bigger until we finally ended up with our family boat, a 48-foot Egg Harbor. But every one of the boats had to be rebuilt. I'd go to my dad's shop, and we would gut them and rebuild them.

I have two brothers; they're both mechanics. My middle brother, Greg, is a transmission specialist for Ford, and my youngest brother, Gary, actually owns his own shop with twelve bays in Micco and lives in Grant, Florida. My father moved back to Miami. His family was originally from the Coral Gables/Homestead area. That was where he grew up.

We always fished, mostly on the ocean. I did some net fishing in the river and a lot of pompano net fishing in my late teens and early twenties, back when it was still legal. I charter fished and I net fished. I really hadn't built my business up much in my early years. I worked for my family, my dad's construction business, up until the time I was twenty-one. And then I just started fishing full time—pompano fishing, mackerel fishing, and whatever else it took to make a living.

CHARTER FISHING

I began working as a mate and just working in the boatyards. I worked for a company out of Sebastian for a while called Treasure Coast Lady. I worked at his fish house, cutting fish and running his charter boat. It was called *TC Lady*. They had the fish house up on the hill right there at the Sebastian River Bridge. That was a restaurant, fish house, and tackle store. I did everything from cutting fish, selling fish, cooking, working the tackle store, and running the charter boat. Whatever it takes. But I just knew I wanted to fish. I grew up in the construction business and knew I did not want to be in that business.

There's another great story. When I was eighteen, my dad showed up on the construction job site one day and handed me a piece of paper and said, "Son, you're going to Palm Beach tonight to start studying for your captain's license." My dad actually came to the job site and had paid for me to go get my captain's license. He just showed up one day and said, "This afternoon you're due in Palm Beach to go start your captain's license." It was at Palm Beach Atlantic College. They were having some courses there to get your captain's license.

PALM BEACH ATLANTIC COLLEGE

My father knew how much I enjoyed fishing. He knew I did not enjoy construction. I worked at construction because I had to. But my love was in the ocean. So I was off to Palm Beach Atlantic College. At the time it was a very tiny school. It was just a captain's course that someone had rented some space for at Palm Beach Atlantic College. It was not the Chapman School [of Seamanship in Stuart, Florida]. This was actually Sea School. This was the early days of Sea School, that's based out of St. Petersburg now. I got a fifty-ton Master Mariner's license. With it, you can run any vessel up to fifty tons, inspected or uninspected. It's just the next step above the six-pack license. I was eighteen. You know, my dad surely wanted me to be in the construction business, but he knew that my heart was not in that. It just seemed natural.

CANOE FISHING

I grew up surfing. I surfed constantly. I was always either surfing or fishing. If there was no surf I would paddle the canoe around, kingfishing, cobia fishing, or tarpon fishing off the beach.

I lived about twelve miles from the beach, and I would ride my bike to the beach every day, twelve miles each way. I lived in Palm Bay, and the closest beach was at Indiatlantic. So I had to ride up through Melbourne, over the Melbourne Causeway, and out through Indiatlantic to get to the beach.

I surfed on a little surf team sponsored by Dick Catree at the time. He is a charter captain in Sebastian today, but at the time he owned a surf shop there called Shag Surf Shop, and he always had surfboards there for me, as well as two canoes, fishing rods, coolers of ice, and everything for us to fish as well. It was a great deal while growing up.

We caught everything from those canoes. We caught kingfish, cobia. I caught a wahoo one time. Those big fish would drag and pull you all around. It was great. I had a tarpon jump in the boat. We were sitting there fishing at the time, and there was a large school of pogies. So we'd take a weighted snag hook and snag the pogies and let them sink. Well, I snagged a pogie and next thing I know, I had about a hundred-pound tarpon laying in the canoe with me. It rolled the canoe over. I mean, it made a mess. Luckily, I kept the rod in my hand, and he broke off. I was able to roll the canoe back over, climb in the canoe, and bail the canoe out. I was by myself snagging pogies. It's a menhaden or, basically, an ocean shad.

As soon as I snagged that pogie, the tarpon jumped. It ate the pogie, and it jumped and it landed in the boat crossways across the canoe. I don't even think he knew what happened. He just ate the bait and ended up landing sideways on the canoe. And I don't think he tipped it over. I think I tipped the canoe over [laughs]. It was pretty funny. Everybody saw it from the beach, and everybody was laughing. It weighed probably about a hundred pounds. Oh, that was great. Yeah, that was a great day.

It's neat when those big fish pull you. It's like one on one. I mean, you're really doing battle with him. I think one of the biggest challenges is, if you want to take that fish, is getting it in the canoe. I've caught numerous forty-pound kingfish out of the canoe, and forty- to fifty-pound cobias.

Now picture being in that little narrow canoe and with a little hand gaff and looking over at this fish eyeball to eyeball, figuring out how you're going to get him in this canoe in front of you without tipping over. That was the biggest challenge—not catching him so much as it was putting them in the boat, landing them. It would take forty-five minutes or better to tire out a fish like that. And I'll tell you, our preferred method was to fight the fish for a long time, and then lead him to the beach with the canoe, beach the canoe, and get out and pull the fish up to the surf. That was our preferred method of landing them.

But there were times when you were a mile offshore. A lot of times in the summertime there's a west wind, and it blows you offshore, and you're not able to get the canoe to the beach. Then you have to take the fish, just wear him down to where they weren't kicking anymore, and put them in the canoe. Just wear them out to nothing, because if you put a hot fish in that canoe with you, it's not pretty, especially in the little aluminum canoe.

Oh, yes, it's truly a lot of fun. That's why you see the popularity of the kayak fishing now. It's just a lot of fun. Kayak fishing in the Indian River Lagoon would be a lot of fun. Plus, the river is just teeming with life right now, teeming. I don't know that you could make a cast right now without catching a jack or a ladyfish or something else.

CHANGES IN CHARTER FISHING

Oh, boy, charter fishing has really changed; it's changed a lot. When I first started charter fishing as a mate, a full-day trip was $250, and you would have everybody. You'd have a bunch of guys and their buddies show up with pickup trucks and garbage cans, and they'd expect to catch five, six hundred pounds of fish a day, between kingfish, grouper, snapper, amberjacks. I mean, it was expected that you'd fill your fish box. And they literally showed up with pickup trucks with big garbage cans in the back to take home their fish.

The boats were very simple. A 30-footer was considered a large boat at that time. The average speed would have been 12 to 15 knots. We had Pacemakers, Egg Harbors, just all kinds of stuff. Boats were much smaller and slower back in those days. There were a lot of wood boats. Yeah, a lot of high-end homemade boats and older Hatterases, the old-style Hatterases. That was all of our earlier charter boats.

Then we started having some faster boats. Jim Smith actually built some of the faster boats in the world. He was from the Treasure Coast. He actually built those boats here on the Treasure Coast. He was building some of the world's fastest boats right there on the river in Sebastian. They built a 60-foot express boat that would run 35 knots in the '70s, which was unheard of. A lot of the development of boats came from this area. Now some of the finer boat builders are in Stuart.

Today, we're getting $1,350 for a full-day charter; we were getting $250 for a full day back in those days. Today my generator probably costs more than what the boats cost back then. Ten thousand dollars would have bought a first-class boat. I remember my father bought our 33 Pacemaker that we had, and I think he spent $6,500 on it, which at the time seemed like a lot of money. Then we brought that thing back to the shop, tore everything out, and rewired it, rebuilt the motors, and built it to what we expected it to be. And every Friday afternoon, we would get off work and we would disappear and go to the marina and stay there until Sunday night. Every weekend. Every single weekend.

Captain Glenn Cameron's *Floridian*.

THE *FLORIDIAN*

In the tournament world that I live in today, this boat, the *Floridian*, is actually average to below average in size. This is a 57-footer. A million dollars is a low-end side. A boat like this today is more like a tractor. It's very simple. There is not a lot in it. It's built for daily use. The typical boat would be more yacht-like and would cost you an average of about two million dollars. It's not uncommon for guys to get five to six million dollars wrapped up in a fishing boat today. I have two 800-horsepower engines in it. It cruises at 30 knots.

FIRST *FLORIDIAN*

My first boat, the first *Floridian,* I actually built myself. It was that Crusader hull that had been stretched out. They stretched that hull out a little bit for pot hauling. It was actually a Crusader mold that somebody here had built a mold off of. There was a company that had the mold up the street, on Old Dixie Highway. So I contracted them to build the hull. Well, the guy was so friggin' drunk that he couldn't even get it together to get it done. So he says, "Here. Here's the mold. Lay the thing up yourself if you want it."

So I hired two guys from the Pursuit factory and bought the resin and the cloth. The three of us laid that boat up over the course of three nights. I had to work the day the boat came out of the mold, so I wasn't there. My wife was there, and she took pictures of it.

I competed in a lot of fishing tournaments around Florida with that

Captain Glenn Cameron (*center*), first mate Kevin Paul (*right*), and a charter waiting for a big bite on an early *Floridian*.

boat. Oh, it was bottom-end compared to other tournament fishing boats, but we won a lot of tournaments with that boat.

SECOND *FLORIDIAN*

My second *Floridian* was still low-end compared to the fleet. I bet you my boat didn't cost half as much as one of the average motors for the other boats. The second *Floridian* was a 39 Monroe.

MATES

I hired local kids for mates in tournaments, local kids that were around here that wanted to work, the ones that looked or seemed ambitious. It takes a lot of work to mate, so your average kid couldn't do the job. But somebody who came from fishing and wanted to fish would die to do this job. It takes a lot of extra . . . you've got to first be competitive as hell. Second of all, you have to love to fish.

One of my best first mates is a first mate on international tournament boats. He's probably one of the best and most sought-after mates in the world, Kevin Paul. In this day and time, he is probably one of the most sought-after mates on the planet.[1]

He came to me fresh out of jail; literally, the day he got out of jail he

---

1 Kevin Paul is the son of Captain Moby Paul, my old friend and captain. Moby taught me how to kingfish.

Mates Tim Lanahan and Roberto Velazquez and Captain Glenn Cameron at the Fort Pierce fuel dock. They are emptying all of their reels of old line and replacing them with new

came down. I was working on my Monroe boat. I had sucked the valve, and I had the head off, and I was replacing the head, the valve, and the cylinder kit that night so I could go out and fish the next day. He came down that afternoon and helped me all night long so I could get out the next day.

At the time, I was running a single-man charter boat, so I gave him the opportunity just to come ride along and see what he thought about it. And the rest is history. I couldn't get rid of him. The first few months, he came along and fished for tips. And then later on he became so valuable to me that I needed him to stick around. He's made a career of charter fishing and sport fishing as a professional mate. These guys, the good mates, can make well over $100,000 a year.

MY FIRST BOATS

My first boats were certainly substandard. If you had to set a standard for tournament billfish boats, I was at the absolute bottom of the scale.

I would be the worst boat in the fleet. The observers in the tournament didn't even want to get on my boat. I mean, they would literally start backpedaling. They'd see me wheel up to the dock to pick up an observer, and they'd start backpedaling. They wouldn't want to get on my boat. But we won. We won every major event here. I've won every major event in the Treasure Coast area, all on my substandard boats.

BIG TOURNAMENTS

The big tournaments, let's start from the beginning with the Finest Kind Quickie. That's held out of Stuart. It's followed up by the Pirate's Cove Sailfish Classic and Stuart Sailfish Club Light Tackle Tournaments. These are all sailfish tournaments held in Stuart that my boat would have been substandard for.

We've won the Finest Kind tournament four times, more than any boat in history. Nobody else has ever done that. We've won the Pirate's Cove Sailfish Classic three times. The three tournaments that I'm talking about are all right in December, back-to-back, with a day in between each tournament. The third one is the Stuart Light Tackle Tournament, which has gone on for fifty-some-odd years. I believe I won that one three or four times, too. We actually won it on their fiftieth year, and that was four or five years ago.

MENTORS

I grew up with some great local fishermen. I grew up with Chip Schafer as a mentor. I just didn't think anybody could catch that many sailfish. I remember being a kid, listening to Chip post these unbelievable catches. I was, like, how? I was out there fishing by him. I caught *a* sailfish. How did he catch fourteen? So he set the bar. We're wondering, "Okay, how do we do this? How do we do it?" And then, not only that, "How do we improve on top of what he's done?" We just kept raising the quality of our presentation.

We developed the dredge. He kind of came in at the tail end of the dredge. A dredge is basically the old umbrella rigs. And we would sweet stack them. We started with the simple four-arm umbrella rig, from back in the days of kingfishing, where you put the tubes on them. Well, we took the tubes off and we started snapping natural mullet baits on them. We started with four arms with four baits. And then we went to a four-arm spreader bar with a chain in the middle of it. And then today's become this conglomeration of four and five bars, with six arms and some of them are three-foot around, and some of them are back to just a foot around.

There are no hooks on them; they're simply teasers for attractions. They are to captivate the interest of the sail and keep them from leaving. Once they get up in that thing, they don't leave until you put a hook in them. They come and stick around. Sailfish, most all fish, are very curious.

It's funny, too, because a lot of the lazier guys use rubber stuff for teasers. Well, it's great for seeing a fish, but they don't stay with it. Fish figured it out pretty quick. Like, the rubber mullets and the rubber shads and these strip teasers, they call them, with the hologram fish on it, well, fish, out of curiosity, will swim up and take a look at that but will almost instantaneously swim away, because it doesn't hold their interest. They see that this isn't real. This is not what they're after.

But when they get up in there with the natural baits that we make here, the mullet mostly, they nose on them. That beak is a big sensor. If you really take a good look at it, that whole thing is full of nerve endings. So they really get up in there, and they get a good feel of what's going on.

The dredge. We got the ideas for these more elaborate dredges from Captains Chip Shafer and Ron Lane (both were respected charter captains in Fort Pierce in the early 1970s, and today Ron Lane is the senior captain of NASCAR's marine fleet out of Daytona Beach). Chip and Ron Lane would fish more chains. They would use squid with the chain, with six squids in line and a mullet in the back, or five mullets in the line, or something like that. That was the early days of what they were doing. And then we took it to the next level, which was the dredge bars and dredge bars with a chain on top of it, and it became just a whole 'nother ball game.

THE PELICAN YACHT CLUB SAILFISH TOURNAMENT

Then there's still the Pelican Yacht Club Sailfish Tournament here in Fort Pierce. That one eluded me for years. I had umpteen gazillion seconds and thirds in that. I mean, I can remember fishing the boat by myself with just one or two other anglers with no mate, and we were getting seconds and thirds in them. But it eluded me for the longest time. I finally won it about ten or eleven years ago. We've won it numerous times since then. But that one just eluded me for a long time. That was one I always wanted, because that's my hometown tournament.

And then for the last six or eight years, we had the Fort Pierce Billfish Derby, which I've won three times. And then we have the Pink Lady's Tournament, for lady anglers here, which I've won two times in the last four years that it's been held. That's held right here at Fort Pierce City Marina.

MOST MEMORABLE TOURNAMENT

I think the most memorable tournament I ever won is when I took my Monroe boat to Palm Beach. I took a local fellow from here, Hans Kraas, who's an international angler. We went down to go fish the Buccaneer Cup, which is a super-prestigious Palm Beach tournament. It's super-prestigious. But we went down there in my little single-engine boat. It was the first year that they added the two-to-one points for trolling. So they accepted the trolling. We went on down there. They accepted the trollers along with the live-baiters. Live-baiting is easier to catch a sail, as opposed to trolling a dead bait. It was the first year that they added the point system where it is two hundred points for a dead-bait sail, and one hundred points for a live-bait sail. So, in order to take advantage of that, we took the boat down and competed in the tournament.

They had a lot of holes in their tournament rules, so I brought a legal pad down to the captains' meeting with all the questions that I had about the holes in their rules. And they actually took me off to the side and said, "No more questions." But I want everybody to hear the discrepancies. There were discrepancies in the rules, which I wanted everybody to know, but they actually took me off to the side and said, "Don't worry about it. Don't worry about it."

I said, "When I win your tournament, I don't want there to be any questions."

So we went down there and won the tournament on my single-engine boat, trolling against an all-live-bait fleet. So they weren't happy with us.

The next year they outlawed single-engine boats, and they outlawed my dredges. I guess it was because we went down there and won. It just seemed awful funny that the next season my dredges were outlawed, and single-engine boats were outlawed. That was probably about 1995.

Well, we were the underdogs for a long time. Oh, then it was funny. When I got this boat, they were saying you're done. Once you got a big, fancy boat you won't win any more tournaments. And then we went out and had our best season ever last year [2009]. My first year on this boat, we had one of our best seasons ever. We just won everything.

WEATHER

I've seen some horrible weather, weather that people don't ever want to see. I can remember, in the last decade or so, we started fishing the other side of the Gulf Stream line, north of the Bahamas. We do it a lot, especially with this boat. I mean, it's not uncommon for us to come back with a thousand, twelve hundred pounds of tunas and big gaffer dolphins. But we're fishing over on the east side of the Stream a lot now.

And I can remember one day my radio goes off with a weather warning. Now, I'm seventy miles offshore, and my marine radio goes off with a weather warning, which, I'm so far out, I shouldn't be able to hear anything. And, you know, it's perfectly blue, awesome skies over where we are. You can't see anything.

So we finish up our day of fishing and we start steaming back. And all of the sudden, the world goes black back to the west where we're going. It looks like we're going right into the gates of hell. There's one opening right in the middle that looks kind of clear. There's three waterspouts on either side of this opening, and there's lightning cracking everywhere, I mean, absolutely everywhere.

I was actually in my Torres boat, and I told everybody, "Let's lash everything down. We're going to pull up in this, and we're just going to slow down and ride it out."

Well, we get in it, and it's got to be blowing 60–70 miles an hour. It pops my curtains free up on my bridge, and all of my isinglass starts popping free. I'm trying to lash all that stuff down. I've got a soft top on it, and the soft top lifted up. I mean, the boat's almost starting to feel light, because it's got lift now from the top being held up.

About this time I hear the Coast Guard calling me on the radio and asking me to keep my eye open for an airplane that just disappeared near me. They're talking to me on the radio, and keep in mind, at this point, I'm fifty miles offshore, and they're able to talk to me because they saw an airplane came in behind where I was and disappeared in the storm. It just disappeared off the radar. The storm was so dense that they just lost the airplane in the storm. I mean, it blew so hard, it blew the ocean flat.

Well, they asked me to redirect, so I ended up redirecting south a ways, and we spent an extra hour-and-a-half looking around. And then, after a while, they finally called me back and said, "Oh, we picked them back up. Thank you for helping. You may continue on." Luckily, the airplane didn't go down.

It blew the ocean flat. I mean, it was just a complete whiteout. It blew so hard that the waves didn't even have a chance to build by us. Everything was just white, just a big foam ball. I mean it was blowing 60–70 miles an hour. It lasted for a good hour and change. We were glad to see that one leave.

LOST PONTOON BOAT

I mean, think about the thunderstorms you see out here all the time. I can remember another time out here. We had been getting some very severe afternoon thunderstorms out here off Fort Pierce. I'm fishing the offshore bar, which is the reef twelve miles off here, and up pulls an aluminum pontoon boat, and it's 12:30 in the afternoon. I'm live-baiting on the reef there, catching some king mackerel. I pull up to him, and I pointed back west and showed him the big thunderheads.

I said, "If I was you, I would start making my way home."

The guy basically flipped me off, told me to mind my own f-ing business. So I went off fishing. That was the last time that boat was ever seen. God, this was way back when I owned the *Breakwater*. Apparently, the pontoon boat broke up. They never found the guys.

I mean, the guy flipped me off, and I'm begging, "Look, dude, it's been blowing 50 to 60 miles an hour in the afternoon for thirty minutes at a crack. If I were you, I'd start making my way home." But think of it, an aluminum pontoon boat!

LOST FISHERMEN

There was another time in the late '80s, early '90s. We were in the *Breakwater* catching bait when we saw a couple of guys in at 10 Buoy. It was early in the spring, and we were having some nasty thunderstorms. They already had their life jackets on, and my mate, Todd Hendrickson, and I, at the time, we're looking at these poor guys catching bait and thinking, "Boy, they don't look like the hardiest." Well, they muddle out there, and one of those thunderstorms popped up, and that was the last anyone saw of them.

Oh, these people just underestimate the power of these afternoon thunderstorms. I mean, it's unbelievable. If one of those storms catches you off guard, and you let yourself get compromised, it will send you down in a heartbeat. Not to mention the lightning mixed in it and the waterspouts and the torrential downpours mixed with 60-, 70-mile-an-hour winds.

LIGHTNING

I've been struck by lightning twice, once at the dock, once in the ocean. It wiped out my electronics and pumps both times. Never had it hurt anybody, but it certainly did a lot of damage. It's far-reaching damage, from every pump on the boat, right on down to your clutch cables and throttle cables. It took a month or two for the burnt clutch cables and stuff to quit working.

I've certainly heard of stories about lightning blowing holes in the ocean, but I have not seen it myself. I've seen lightning electrify the surface. Usually, I'm ducking. I let go of everything just in case it strikes the boat.

BLUEFIN TUNA

We have some awesome pictures of some bluefin tunas that we've caught. We've got some just amazingly big bluefins. The actual weights are unknown, because we sold them as cores. We ship them to Japan. When we were fishing in New England and we would catch them and then cut the throat latch, cut the tube, the ass tubes. Then you hydro gun them and scrub them out. Then you put them in an ice vat and drop the temperature, rice paper them, and overnight them to Japan.

We caught some fish over a thousand pounds. That's the plug itself, just the body cavity with no head, tail, guts, or anything. It would weigh 750 to 800. Initially, you didn't cut the heads off. You ship them with the head on. Ship them with the head and part of the tail, so that they can carry them. It helps take care of the fish. And actually, they want to see the eye of the fish to judge its freshness. But once that fish is sold, they cut the head off.

When we were commercial tuna fishing in a 43-foot Merritt, there was two of us, Dave Berrard and myself. I think a long fight was twenty minutes. We were fishing with the 130 reels, 130 Internationals, with the unlimited stand up and unlimited bent rods. And we'd put a hundred pounds, 140 pounds of pressure on them and back the boat up as hard as we could on them. It was a fifteen- to twenty-minute battle, and it was over.

If it took you longer than that, it would burn the fish up. They would get what they call lactic acid in the fish, which would give the meat a rainbow sheen, which was undesirable for the Japanese. That tainted the meat. So you wanted to keep the lactic acid down. The longer you fought the fish, the more it was stressed, and the more rainbow sheen or lactic acid buildup throughout the meat, thus dropping the price. So you wanted to catch that fish as fast as possible.

It was a charter fisherman that introduced me to commercial tuna fishing, and this was before I bought my first charter boat. I was hired to go in late summer, which was, or is, our off-season. But it is the prime season for bluefin tuna fishing. So I went there in the off-season and mated for a local charter fisherman from Stuart. It was a great time. You were allowed one fish a day. I think we caught twenty-two fish for the season, which was an incredible thing to do. Here we were a Florida boat, and we went to New Hampshire and Maine as a Florida boat. They just figured we didn't know shit. But we got up there and ended up doing exceptionally well, especially by comparison to the other boats that were catching tuna fish. We were high hooks there. It's an incredible fishery.

TUNA ACROSS THE GULF STREAM

A friend of mine, Eddie Dwyer, started doing it here. Ed Dwyer is a friend of mine who I met up on the Space Coast, when I lived in Palm Bay and Melbourne. I met Ed back in the early '80s, when he moved here from Ohio. He became a charter captain out of the Port Canaveral area.

And being up there, he would go to lunch and meet the guys that were working at the Space Center. He was talking to these fellows that were recovering space missile parts and shuttle parts and all that. He started talking to them about the birds they were marking on their radar, of all things. So that intrigued him. And they were talking about all these schools of tuna that were over on the other side of the Gulf Stream they saw by radar on the ships that were doing the recovery of the space shuttle debris.

So he thinks, they saw all these birds and tunas out there. So Eddie decided he was going to go there and check it out. Well, the rest is history. He developed one hell of a fishery over there. So Ed developed that fishery, and I mean, the early-season fishery there is incredible. I mean, when we first started doing it, it was nothing to catch eighteen or twenty tunas, a blue marlin or two, a boxful of thirty-, forty-, and fifty-pound dolphins. As a matter of fact, my son, Nicky, caught a sixty-some-pound dolphin over there.

But the fishing over there is just remarkable. It was like virgin fishing territory. It really, really was like virgin fishing there and still is. I mean, the fishing is far enough away that it doesn't get too much pressure. It's becoming more and more popular today. But because it's a sixty-, seventy-mile ride, it's still not overfished. It's a little over a two-hour ride over. It's not bad in this boat. In an outboard boat, it's not that much fun, I would think. I mean, the guys do it all the time, but I don't recommend it because of the storms that you can hit. But it's an incredible fishery.

BIG FISH

A 1,012-pound blue marlin out of Virginia back in the '80s was my biggest fish. And I've caught numerous big bluefins. Out of Fort Pierce I think I caught a 440-pound blue marlin. That would have been my largest one ever here, and that's very large for here. You don't see very many of them bigger.

FIRST BIG BLUE MARLIN

I think it was in '79 or '80, in an old Summit Landings Tournament. It was at the Neptune Marina, in Sebastian. It later became Summit Landings. It's just on the north side of the Sebastian River. I was fishing on my family boat back then. A 453-pound marlin.

It was in the early days, before we really knew what we were doing. We were fishing with a wire leader and real light hooks, but we decided we were going to put a big lure in front of a ballyhoo. So we were in about 130 foot of water, and it's late in the day and kind of stormy and rainy. I'm driving the boat, and my dad's asleep. My buddy's back there fishing, and my brother's asleep. All of a sudden, a rigger goes off, and I look back, and there's this big-ass blue marlin jumping back there.

My dad's asleep. I wake him up, and I said, "Dad! We have a blue marlin on!"

He starts laughing and says, "Son, you probably just saw a porpoise" [laughs].

But anyway, after about an hour and a half, this thing pops up there, and everybody's like, "Holy shit, you're right!"

So we finally put it in the boat, and we win the tournament—this is actually up there in Sebastian—but we finally caught him and subdued him and put him in the boat and ended up winning the tournament.

But I thought it was really funny that everybody was asleep, and they thought I was out of my mind when I said we had a blue marlin on. We were in such shallow water and it was such an uncommon occurrence that they thought I was crazy. Biggest fish wins. In that particular tournament, the biggest fish wins.

CATCHING BIG FISH

Today, we go to a little island called Rum Key, which is about 400 miles southeast of Fort Pierce. We've caught numerous fish in the eight- and nine-hundred-pound range out there, numerous marlins. I like to fish with the lighter gear, so we were catching them with International 50s or Tiagra 50s with some other fifty- and sixty-pound line. You back up on them, and your drag is fairly light. With sixty-pound line, we're probably fishing eighteen pounds of drag.

When the fish goes off jumping, I immediately go into a turn. I kind of follow him up for a while. You get everything cleared up on deck. Once everything's cleared up, I back up on the line itself and chase the fish backwards while the guy's reeling down on it to get as much line in as you can. And then they're in the fighting chair.

We caught one that measured 960-something there, and we actually spent 3½ hours with that one. We lose those big ones frequently, and it seems a lot of times you lose as many as you catch, especially when you're lure fishing. If you catch half the fish that bite lure fishing, you've done pretty well. We do use some bait, but we also often pull some lures.

One of the greatest ways in the world to get a blue marlin is by pulling lures, but it's also one of the greatest ways to lose a fish. With lures your hookup ratios aren't that good. You've got this big-headed lure-and-hook setup, and it just seems like, with all the crap that's on there, you just end up pulling a lot of them off. It's just the nature of having to pull such a large bait to try to hook a fish. It is just the equation to pull them off. And then we're using fairly light tackle, and it's hard enough to pull the bait in with nothing on it.

Sometimes it takes that larger bait to get the bite. And then since we're fishing a little bit lighter gear, our hooks are a little bit smaller than if we were pulling 80s or 130s. So our hooks are a little bit smaller so that you can penetrate the mouth of the fish with the lighter drag. The whole equation is just a great way to pull a fish off. It's a great way to get a bite, but also a great way to lose them.

But in the end it's worth it, because you can stand up and fight them, and it's just more challenging. And you're letting them go anyway; we release them. Rather than sitting in the fighting chair, you can stand up with a belt and a harness and fight it, which is something that we're real big on—stand-up fighting. That way, you really get the feel of the fight. My charters seem to like that a lot better. And my guys like the lighter gear.

WEIRD RIPS

I've certainly seen some god-awful rips and stuff, being that we fished out here all winter long in some of the most horrible weather that you can ever imagine. When you get on those Gulf Stream rips, sometimes it'll be one foot on one side, and you cross into that rip, and it's eight and ten foot on the other side. I remember hooking a fish, fishing in the rough stuff, and then swinging into the calm stuff to fight the fish.

It's just off here in the Gulf Stream that the Gulf Stream some-times gets really rough in the middle of winter, when you see all those humps off there on the horizon. A lot of times that is on an absolute finite break, and it's usually offshore of where the guys go kingfishing. But, I mean, it could be a foot or two inside and then just "victory at sea" on the outside. It's just amazing, the force that that current has bucked up against that northwester or north wind.

When the Gulf Stream current is going north, and the wind is com-ing out of the north and mixed in with a long-period ground swell, it gets crazy. Inside it, it only seems like it's a foot, but there may be five foot of heave, with a one-foot chop on it. But you don't notice the five-foot heave out of the current. But once that five foot of heave and that one foot of chop in that Gulf Stream current, with that north wind bucking into it, it amplifies it. So it takes that five foot of heave, turns it into eight foot, and that one foot of chop is now three or four foot of white water on top of it.

KINGFISH IN THE DEEP

Kingfish are often well offshore of the bar. Typically, the fish are on that reef at 90 to 100 feet. But when those fish are moving, they are not stuck to that reef. They move around.

I can remember fishing a tournament one year, and I called George Kaul. I said, "Look, I just marked an acre of kingfish here. I just went through it. It clipped all my shit off, and I kept going."

George didn't believe me.

And I said, "George, I'm in 120 foot of water. It's a good place to fish."

But Tommy Jones said, "Okay, I'll come out there and check it out, Sneakerhead."

So he rolled right out there, put it in a circle, and caught his limit and left. And I think everybody that came off out there that day caught their limit.

Damn, I find them out there quite frequently like that. The kingfishermen listen now. I've caught kingfish off there in 150 foot on some wrecks where you can just smash them. I've caught them off there in 160 foot on some of the natural bottom off the northeast.

Captain Ron Lane showed me that back in October, two decades ago, when they weren't really on that reef. You'd get off there on those offshore rocks, and there's huge mounds of bait, and the kingfish are just stacked up. It's three miles off the Northeast Grounds, in the 320s, about three miles from the 320s on the reef, to the 320s on twenty-seven fathoms. In the summer and fall of the year, it seems like they're off there more. There's rocks out there, too, where we're catching red snappers.

RESCUES

Probably one of the best ones was early in my career, when I was out of Sebastian Inlet. Some fellows had lost power with their 26-foot outboard boat, and the guy's on the radio almost crying. He's scared to death. He's off Wabasso, where the waves break on that outer reef. He had thrown his anchor outside of that, but his anchor didn't hold, and he slid in, and his anchor head caught on the outside of the reef. So his boat is up in the middle of the breaking waves, and he's still a good half-mile or more offshore. These guys are scared to death. It had gotten rough, so I was kind of coming in with my charter fare at the time.

Off Wabasso there's a reef that's a half or three-quarters of a mile offshore. It's similar to what Monster Hole would be at Sebastian Inlet. It's a little bit further offshore than that, even. It's basically that same reef line that you mackerel fish up and down on off of Fort Pierce and Vero. When it gets six foot or better, it breaks on that reef.

The fellow had lost power, thrown his anchor over a mile offshore that drug until he was sitting in middle of the breakers. So he was freaking. He can't swim, so he's afraid to swim to the beach, and he's afraid he's going to lose his boat.

So I take my anchor line and put it all in my cockpit. I surfed and swam a lot, so I had my mate hold my boat just outside the breaking waves and I jumped in with the line tied around my waist. I swim to his anchor line, and I tie a bolo around his anchor line and swim back to my boat. Then we used my anchor line like an anchor ball and pulled his anchor out of the reef, and then pulled him back through the waves.

We got him back into Sebastian. That guy was the happiest guy you ever saw in your life when I got him back inside Sebastian Inlet. I saved his boat and saved him from having to get in the ocean. We've done a lot of different ocean rescues. But that one really stands out in my mind.

LOST DIVERS

When I owned the *Breakwater*, we're coming back in late one afternoon. There's not a boat on the horizon anywhere, and my mate at the time, Todd Hendrickson, and I are sitting up on the bridge, and I see a stick. Now, keep in mind, I'm six to eight miles offshore, and I see a stick start to wave. And this is in the afternoon. A little bit of the afternoon sea breeze has started, and it's kind of choppy.

I slow down and pull up, and there's a diver in the water. Now, we're eight miles offshore and he's got no tanks on. He's just swimming. We get him in the boat, and we come to find out that there was a heavy north current at the time, and he had gotten away from his boat. And

I guess they couldn't get the boat started or something. Anyway, he ended getting swept way north, and he was trying to swim ashore.

He had a buddy with him, but he had given his buddy his tanks and his lobsters. So I picked him up and swung back around, figured out the tide and everything, and how far he had swum. We came back around and somehow came back to his buddy a mile away.

Now, at this point, I'm three miles down the line, and I can actually see his boat at this point. So I ended up steaming three more miles back to the boat, where the girls couldn't get the motor started. They had left their wives on the boat, and the women couldn't get the boat started. They're just bawling. They're sitting on the boat just crying, and they knew they had just lost their husbands.

Well, I come wheeling up with their husbands, with their twenty-four lobsters and all their gear and everything. Well, those guys were trying to give me lobsters, and I looked at them and I said, "Look, guys, you had better keep those lobsters, because I don't think your wives are going to let you dive again for a long time."

RESCUE AT SEBASTIAN INLET

I started my career at Sebastian Inlet. I remember being a surfer at Sebastian, and there was a small aluminum V-hull boat anchored up from the stern on the south side of the south jetty there. It was a really beautiful summer day, with maybe a three-foot ground swell and an incoming tide at the time. The guy had his seven-year-old son and his father and himself in about a 16-foot V-hull aluminum boat anchored from the stern in Sebastian Inlet. It was a beautiful, beautiful day and an incoming tide.

Well, one of my friends was a lifeguard there at the time, and he got his paddleboard and paddled over to the guy. He said, "Look, you need to get out of here. This tide's going to change in thirty-five minutes. Once this tide changes, right here where you're sitting, it's going to be breaking."

The guy cussed him out, told him to get the hell out of there and mind his own business. So my buddy brought his paddleboard back over, and they staged to go rescue these people, because they knew they were going to need to be rescued.

Well, then the tide went slack, and you could see the boat ease up on the anchor. And then it started charging out. It took about five minutes

for that boat to go under. And don't you know, the guy was more worried about his tackle box and his fish rods than he was for his father
and his seven-year-old son. It was unbelievable. But, I mean, the guy
was warned.

We got everybody out of the water, but we wouldn't take his fishing
tackle. They would not. We wouldn't even think about it. The boat went
right down and got drug out to sea, and the last thing I saw was the bow
of that little boat disappearing.

CUBAN RAFTS

I've seen a million Cuban rafts. That actually was a great time. When
the Cuban rafts were coming through, we caught a lot of big dolphins
off those things. We found numerous boats.

LOST KITE

I found a kite from a kite board out there one time.[2] Moby Paul's son,
Brian Paul, was here, and I brought this thing in, this tangled mess.
We figured it was a kite of some kind. I ended up giving it to Brian,
and Brian untangles it. He gets the serial number off of it and ends up
finding the guy who owned it out of Palm Beach. The guy had actually
let go of it off Palm Beach, and I found it up off of Sebastian out in the
middle of the Gulf Stream. And Brian Paul tracked the guy down and
got the guy's kite back to him.

LOST ZODIAC

We were just coming home, and I found this Zodiac floating and towed
it in. Come to find out, the guy had lost it off Bimini. I actually pulled
it in here. I called the Coast Guard, the Coast Guard contacted the guy,
and the guy ended up coming here to the City Marina in Fort Pierce
and picking up his Zodiac.

That was a really good one, because the guy was a professional captain.
He was a South African captain for a boat, and he had had his friends
on the boat in Bimini. They weren't supposed to be on the boat, and his
friends didn't tie up this Zodiac very well. This South African captain
was very likely going to lose his job if he didn't get this Zodiac back. It
was a very nice Zodiac. He was very happy to get his Zodiac back.

---

2 A kite is a parachute-type device used by kite surfers. It's used for high-speed surfing on
windy days.

MESSAGE BOTTLES

In Rum Key, we find bottles from all these school ships. We find them, and my son has actually replied to a lot of them. For some reason, the currents just wash all this stuff at Rum Key. We've found three or four bottles with messages in them there from school ships traveling the Caribbean that have released these bottles and wanted to know where they ended up. It's pretty neat.

OTHER BUSINESS

I've had some people drinking and getting out of line on the boat. I really don't like people drinking all that much when we're out there fishing, and I try to quell all that.

I've seen some bad things happen with some of the guys smuggling people and smuggling drugs. I've kept that as far away from me as I possibly can. I really enjoy being in that ocean. I can't imagine being locked in a cell.

I have always had one of the really busiest charter businesses. And I've seen some people with half my business all of a sudden come up with these really nice boats and start having other people do work on them in the boatyard. And I'm standing there asking the question, "Wow, how can you afford this?"

They say, "Oh, well, you know the charter business."

"Really?" I'm thinking to myself, "I must be doing something wrong." And then a handful of months later, there are these big federal indictments and prison time for these guys.

I can think of one incident here, about five years ago, where a guy had just gotten in the business, and the next thing you know, he was jammin', doing really well. The charter business has been good, but I could never afford to have other people do work on my boat. If I was going to paint my boat, or if I was going to do some major work, I would always have to do it myself, because there was never the money there to have all this work done.

Well, next thing I know, this guy got a second boat, and he's going back and forth to the Bahamas constantly. He's telling me he's got all these charters to the Bahamas, which was something that I had been trying to do, but I could never really put it all together. And the next thing I know, he's in the boatyard with these two boats and has got all this work going on. Three months later, he gets busted for smuggling, smuggling people and smuggling cocaine. And now he's in prison for life.

Stuff like that really tells you to stay the hell away from it, no matter how great the intrigue is for the big money and all that. If you don't have your freedom, you don't have anything. You can't put a price on that.

BODIES

I found some people from a plane wreck out here one time. We were fishing a weed line, and I first found luggage. And then we saw something, and it just didn't look right. And we pulled up, and it was a woman floating face down. We called the Coast Guard, and we were kind of waiting around. We were just kind of moving around the weed line, fishing, waiting for the Coast Guard to show up, and we actually ended up finding two more bodies. It was kind of creepy. I don't ever want to do that again.

SNEAKERHEAD

One year, the kingfishermen kept talking about all these remoras, catching all these remoras, and those are "sneakerheads." Ah, the kingfish guys were catching a lot of them. It was summertime, and they were catching a bunch of them.

So George Kaul says, "I got all these god-danged remoras."

I said, "They're called sneakerheads, George. It's a sneakerhead."

Ah, George starts laughing out loud, and next thing I know, the next day, he's calling me Captain Sneakerhead.

They're called that because the suction part of the fish looks like the bottom of a tennis shoe. Captain Ron Lane always called them that. You know, I worked as a mate for him some, and I'd fill in for him as a mate, and he always called them a sneakerhead. So, I mean, that's just what I called them, sneakerheads [laughs]. Now the kingfishermen call me Captain Sneakerhead.

COMMERCIAL KINGFISHERMEN

Well, I kind of came from that area. I mean being from Sebastian, I grew up around commercial fishing and fishermen. I worked at Sembler's Fish House, picking fish out of the nets. I've just always been around them. I've always kind of identified with commercial fishermen, more than the normal charter guys you got here.

Here in Florida we get a lot of charter guys that just kind of retire from land jobs in New Jersey. And I've always kind of identified more with the commercial guys than with a lot of the charter guys.

FUNNY STORIES

One guy comes down first thing in the morning and says, "Oh yeah, I was in the navy," and he's carrying a cooler, and we're trying to help him on the boat, and he doesn't need any help. He steps on the boat with his cooler of beer, a Styrofoam cooler of beer, and his foot comes out from underneath him, and he straddles the covering boards right on his balls, and his Styrofoam cooler hits the cover board, shatters, beer and sandwiches go everywhere, and he just kind of folds over like a cartoon character and just falls right in the cockpit [laughs].

Or the one time I was fishing with Captain Ron Lane, and this guy's out fishing, and his wife's puking over the side, and she pukes her false teeth out. She pukes out her false teeth. Her husband's giving her shit, giving her shit, and giving her shit.

So Captain Ron Lane, who's not typically known for humor, looks down and says, "Don't worry. The next fish we catch with a set of dentures, we'll make sure to get them back to you!"

Or one time I'm fishing in Virginia, and we're jigging for sea bass, and this is a bachelor party, and this guy is drunker than Hogan's goat. He's sitting there jigging, and he gets a bite and goes right over the side, and he's got a brand new pair of Ray-Ban sunglasses on. So he disappears. The water's about 58 degrees, and he disappears over the side.

And we're thinking, "Oh, God."

So he finally pops back up. And now he looks sober.

And I go, "Where's the fishing pole?"

And he hands up the fish pole, and it's got two of those big four-pound sea bass, black willies, on that thing. Wheeled him in, and he's upset. He says, "I just bought that pair of sunglasses. Brand-new pair of Ray-Bans."

I'm fishing right beside him, and I get a bite. I crank up. I get a sea bass on the bottom hook, and his Ray-Bans caught right in the middle of the bridge, on my top hook [laughs].

CHARTER CAPTAIN

I absolutely enjoy my life. I wouldn't trade what I do for anything. I'll never be rich by what I do, but the richest people in the world can't do what I do. We've proven that time and time again with my substandard boats, for instance. The richest people in the world are competing against us. But yet, we win time and time again with our boats, just because we grew up doing it.

This is our world. It's not how much money you have or how much fame you've got. It's how much you put into it. There's absolutely no substitute for that. I mean, you get out of something what you put in [laughs]. Period.

One of my friends laughs because I could go fishing all week long, and then he'll call up and want to go river fishing. He'll call me, and I'll just go river fishing with him. His wife says, "Is he insane? He's just fished every friggin' day for a month, and now he's fishing in the river with you?"

But, you know, it's just how much we love it. I mean, you can see it. And the guys that do it and do it well, they love it, I mean. And they do it all the time because they love it, not because they make money at it, but because they love it. Because for the effort that we have to put in to make the little bit of money that we do, you could put in half the effort at something else and take home a whole lot more money. So you just absolutely have to love it. There's no substitute for it.

Captain Glenn, grouper, and happy charter.

5

Captain George Kaul

George Kaul is a legend among Florida commercial hand-line king mackerel fishermen. He is also one of the happiest fishermen. Like the other captains in this book, he is highly competitive. Throughout his career, he has consistently had the biggest catches of kingfish among his peers.

Near the beginning of his commercial fishing career, George averaged between 800 and 900 pounds of kingfish daily. To pull that many fish on a daily basis, by hand, one fish at a time, from dawn to dark, is absolutely amazing—a feat of great physical strength and endurance. George would often fish these long hours for many days on end, including once for seventy days straight.

During the early, "good," years, he wisely invested his fishing profits into building lots, built starter homes, and held the mortgages for the buyers. He capitalized on Florida's building boom.

George talks a lot on the VHF radio when he's fishing. He is usually the main voice people hear when they monitor Channel 19, the commercial fishing channel in the Fort Pierce area. George talks so much that people wonder how he has time to catch all of the fish he catches, and he nearly always catches more fish than anyone else.

Because of his loquaciousness on the radio, George is well known in other circles as well. My friend Richard Green, who sharpens knives for restaurants on the Treasure Coast, listens to Channel 19 while sharpening knives at his home shop west of Fort Pierce. He says George Kaul is so entertaining that he should have been a comedian. During one of George's hospital visits to his mom, a nurse who also fishes heard George's voice and said, "I know you! You're the commercial fisherman that is always on Channel 19."

As Loretta, George's wife, relates it, George was talking on the radio when she hooked a forty-four-pound kingfish on the bug line in Jupiter,

Captain George Kaul and wife Loretta at their home in western Saint Lucie County.

George with grandsons Hunter and Seth.

Florida. She said the fish nearly pulled her overboard before George, after hearing her screams, got off the radio and came to her aid.

For Captain George Kaul, the freedom, independence, and economic opportunity afforded by commercial kingfishing was a perfect fit, especially early on, when he seemed to lack direction. While this could be said of all of the captains in this book, it is especially true of George.

Today, George lives west of Fort Pierce on fifteen acres with a pond teeming with fish. He divides his time between catching king and Spanish mackerel and bluegills and bass fishing with his young grandsons, Hunter and Seth, who have already won several local youth fishing tournaments. Though George doesn't commercial fish as much or as hard as he used to, he still may well be the best commercial kingfish captain alive today.

George Kaul in His Own Words

I was born in East Brunswick, New Jersey, on January 18, 1950. We always fished. My father had bought a wooden boat, and we fished in Sandy Hook. We caught tuna fish, fluke, porgies. There were also little school tunas. We were fishing the acid waters off of Long Island. Acid water was tainted, yellowish water dumped from washing out the bilges of barges offshore. The fish loved it. I was only seven, eight, and nine years old, but I remember it. We have family movies of it. We had a wood Pacemaker.

Today, I have a fiberglass boat, all glass, which is also a Pacemaker, the *Big Chief*. My family's boat was 28 foot. Well, I fished with my father. My brother was only a year or two old, and he would be on board. My sister was a year older, and she would go out with us, too. And we were sport fishermen. But that's how we got our start in the ocean.

My father had a tool-and-die business in New Jersey. He was a machinist and tool-and-die maker. On weekends we would go fishing. A lot of our fishing was trolling. Some of it was bottom-fishing with lead and cut bait. When we fished, basically, the whole family would go, mostly on pretty days, of course, because it was strictly for fun.

And then when I was ten years old, we moved to Jacksonville, Florida, and brought the boat down from New Jersey, and we started to learn about the fishing down here. We kept the boat at Hokes Marina, in Mayport near Jacksonville. They had little fishing tournaments, and we would get in those.

I caught my first sailfish, I think when I was thirteen, in one of those tournaments and got a little trophy for it. So that was the start of my Florida saltwater career, a fishing contest in Jacksonville. Then gradually we would start to catch kingfish there also. We trolled and rigged ballyhoo and mullet. No sea witches or nothing like you do here.

CHUM

There's a big shrimp boat fleet in Mayport. We would meet them coming in and buy thirty-five-gallon garbage cans of chum from them for five or ten bucks. They would fill the thing full of the dead little spots and croakers and stuff. Then we would anchor outside the inlet and set up a little chum slick going. We'd put about a twelve-foot leader on with about a three-inch-diameter cork on it, and just with this dead bait, you'd let your bait out. You'd keep throwing out this chum and let your dead spot on your hook just drift with it. Pretty soon a kingfish would grab it.

George and his father with their catch at Hokes Marina in Mayport, near Jacksonville.

Young George with a jack crevalle, Jacksonville, early 1960s.

George with sailfish, Village of Mayport, near Jacksonville.

George at thirteen with his forty-pound sailfish, a contest winner.

Now, it was strictly on a sport-level basis. We never sold anything then. Just a dead bait within the slick, and we'd catch twenty- to thirty- to forty-pound kingfish. And just keep throwing chum out. You'd get sharks doing this, too. But that's how we caught our first big kingfish here.

It wasn't big in numbers, though. But some days you'd catch maybe four or five or six. Most days, you'd be lucky if you'd catch one or two. But they would be big fish. And that was what the local sport people did. We often caught thirty- to forty-pounders. We never caught one bigger than that.

FORT PIERCE, FLORIDA

In '65, we brought that same boat here to Fort Pierce. I was fifteen at the time. We started out fishing like we did in Jacksonville. But then we'd watch the commercial guys, and my father got intrigued by it and how much easier and faster they would catch fish on hand line, five-to-one more than you would on a rod.

When we first brought our boat down, it was at the Pelican Yacht Club, and then we moved it over to Mel Seiley's Riverside Marina, where I am now. My father got to be friends with Sherman Merritt, who didn't tell you a lot, but he'd tell him a little bit at a time. So we gradually started rigging lines up to commercial kingfish.

At that time there was no licenses or permits. Anybody who caught fish could pull up to the fish houses and sell them. Herman Summerlin had a fish house over on the south causeway where Chuck's Seafood Restaurant is today. And we would take our few fish that we caught over there to Herman. That's where we would sell them for nine or ten cents a pound; it wasn't much. We moved here in '65, and it was probably '67 and '68 when we started learning about kingfishing.

COMMERCIAL FISHING

It was a couple years after we were here that we started the commercial end of it. And after a couple years, we got to where we'd catch six to eight hundred pounds a day, which was not great back then, compared to Roger Farlow's, Steve Lowe's, and Al Tyrrell's catches. They were really the big-time fishermen. If we caught that, then they'd catch two thousand in comparison. But we were learning.

We fished until I went in the service at nineteen. I guess it was 1970. My brother was about twelve, and he started fishing with my father, and, of course, we learned a little more. My father sold the *Georgie Lou* in 1971. That was the name of the wood boat that we brought from Jersey that we'd been fishing all this time. It was getting kind of old because it was a wood boat. So my father bought a glass boat called the *Lou Donna*, which had twin 318 Chrysler gasoline engines. We had it for about a year, year and a half, only. Then my father built up the *Aurora*, which was the 34-foot fiberglass boat. My father had that boat until he quit fishing in the middle '80s. He finally sold it to Craig Jones. After Craig Jones sold it, it became a shark boat, and then I haven't seen it in recent years.

SCHOOL

From the time I was in junior high, my father was impaired and always was on crutches. He had polio when he was young, and he couldn't get around too good, hopping up on a boat, taking lines off, and stuff. So every chance he would get to go fishing, if it was a school day but he had a chance to go fishing, he would ask me, he'd say, "You got anything important in school today?" And of course I always said no [laughs].

He'd say, "Good, we'll go fishing tomorrow."

So we would go fishing. It kind of got me hooked on fishing, and I loved the fishing. I wasn't crazy over school anyway. I did get into numbers and math in school, and history and geography were fun. But English I was very poor at. And literature or anything that had to do with English or spelling was difficult. Just like spelling "*A u r o r a*" [laughs]. I was very poor at spelling. So I was glad to not have to go to school and go fishing.

Then I got out of high school and went to junior college here. Pretty much my first year, I tried. I did average, C average. And then the second year, the first semester, I started not going. And then I just lost interest completely. By the end of the second semester, I didn't enroll back in at all. And then I got a draft notice from the military, and that started my three years in the military, Vietnam and Panama Canal Zone. I enjoyed my service time in the military, and I thought about staying in and making a career out of it.

VIETNAM

After AIT, Advanced Individual Training, which is roughly eight weeks of training in the different training procedures, or the first four months with a leave in between, and then you go right straight to Vietnam. I landed in Cam Ranh Bay. That's where you come in-country and then you disperse out from there.

I was dispersed up into the northern part of the country, to Huong Tre. I spent a lot of my time on the firebases up there, Alpha, Charlie, Bravo, which are right on the DMZ with North Vietnam. We could actually watch the North Vietnamese raise their flag on their little firebase every morning, and they could watch us raise ours. That's how close we were. We could actually see the flags go up and down. And that's where I spent most of my time.

And I was in the Combat Engineers, which our basic job was mine-sweeping, perimeter setup, building roads, clearing firebases, pushing the perimeters back—the jungle back—so you have a clearing and such. We also built the bunkers that everybody lived in. So we had different squads that would do different things on different days.

Every morning, a squad of five would do the minesweep of the road, wherever you are. The bases were small. We did the minesweep on the road from Khe Sahn. We set up another firebase in Khe Sahn, and we did the minesweep from Khe Sahn to the Laos border every morning. That was my unit's job. We would walk that with mine detectors every morning. That's what we did for six weeks. We were ambushed a couple of times. We probably found mines three or four times. We would blow them.

One time we missed the mines, and the main unit comes behind you. You're like a quarter mile ahead of them, doing your minesweeping and making sure everything's clear. And they're from like a quarter mile or so behind you, and we went through and didn't find anything. All of a sudden we hear—BOOM! BOOM!—a couple explosions behind us, and found out we missed a couple of mines. They got the lead vehicles, and then there was a little firefight and ambush.

Once they stop you, then that's when they hit you. But they were not major fights. If we'd miss them, they'd blow up a vehicle or two, and there'd be a little firefight for four or five minutes. Then they would take off and run, because they knew we would call in the air support, and they had no chance then, because they had no air cover or nothing to fight against us with. Once our air support came in, they were dead. Then we just had them dead to rights. They could hide in the jungle and be hard to see, but with our modern technology, we could strafe that jungle good, and so they ran. Their fights were short. And then they would run.

Once when we were patrolling from Khe Sahn to Laos, right before the ARVNs [Army of the Republic of Vietnam] got their butts kicked in Laos, we were sitting there, at the end of our minesweep from Khe Sahn to the Laos border. We sat down and were actually waiting for pickup to go back. We were sitting there, and we were spread out, the five of us spread out. You always disperse; you don't sit in a cluster. You always spread out. And we had two of us on one side of the road spreading and three of us on the other side. We were just sitting there. And all of a sudden, out of the woods, here comes what looked like an ARVN unit. They all looked the same, fatigues and stuff, which, your North Vietnamese fighters, they wore black, with their little straw hats—the real "gooks," what we called them that we fought. But these looked like South Vietnamese soldiers. So I tried a little conversation. They spoke good English. We sat there and talked a second. I was just sitting there, and I had my weapon out of arm's reach. It was lying there maybe six feet from me. I was just sitting there, which was a mistake.

Then I just started wondering, just by the conversation, just because he was asking me questions about how many of us in this unit and what are we waiting for and trying to get information. And I just happen to glance around, and there's one of them on each one of us, but they didn't have any weapons. That's the next thing I noticed, that they had no weapons. So that kind of eased tensions a little bit.

But then, just as quick as they were there and they asked a few questions, they disappeared back into the jungle. They all just backed off and went back into the jungle. So I started thinking. They weren't friendly; they were looking for information. But they didn't care about just trying to knock off the five of us. They had a bigger plan.

I don't remember if it was immediately, the next day, or a couple days later, but that's when the ARVNs got their butts kicked, and they just came storming out of Laos back across the border. We were there doing minesweep. It happened early in the morning. We hadn't even finished our minesweep. We found the whole road was mined. So I think, this was planned by the VC [Viet Cong] and the Laos soldiers.

We found a stretch there of numerous mines, and, at the same time, all hell breaks loose across the border and all the ARVNs and the South Vietnamese soldiers returning, because we couldn't cross the border. The South Vietnamese soldiers that we had trained were the ones that went across. There're trucks, and everybody was running, storming back. We tried to stop them, because the roads were all mined, but they wouldn't stop. They just ran through the mines, and they were blowing up all over.

I think we got to blow up some before it happened. We blew up one mine, and they were set for contact when the truck tire runs over it. And then—shoop! You press it down, there's a click, and as long as you stay on it, you're okay. When you release the pressure, that's when it blows. Antipersonnel or these bigger mines that were set for the trucks and stuff, that's the way they would operate, too. As long as you kept the pressure down, once you set it, you're okay. But once you release it—pblttt!

SURVIVING IN VIETNAM

In the beginning, it was slow, but then, after you just get used to it and you just take it like another day, like, it's a job. And you never thought about it. In the beginning, you're all tense and not knowing, but then, with the veterans that were there, you get mingled in with them and you realize, it's just the flow of life. And you can't stop what's going to happen. You know if it happens, you're not going to know when it happens, and you just learn to live with it and just go on.

MY PURPLE HEART

There was a big buildup of North Vietnamese soldiers. So we were reinforcing these little firebases. We didn't know what was going to happen, if there was some kind of thing that would come across the border from North Vietnam, with North Vietnamese regulars or what. So we were on these firebases, and probably half a dozen times a day, we would get incoming. We'd get hit with six to eight rounds, mortars, B-22 rockets, and then everything would get quiet. That's when everybody'd get out, get back to work. Two hours later, an hour and a half later, here comes another half a dozen mortars and B-22 rockets, and you basically lived with that every day.

That's the way it was. They'd just raise a little havoc and get whatever they hit, because they know you go underground, and you're safe from that size of the mortars in the bunkers we built. Basically, if you're inside, you're safe.

One day I heard the first mortar, the first rocket or mortar go over. I don't remember now which it was. As long as you hear the whistle, you're safe. As long as you hear the whistle of it going through the air, that means it's already over you and going past you, and it's just going to land on the other side of you. It's what you don't hear you got to worry about. So I heard the whistle of the first one go over. But that's the warning sign. There's another half a dozen coming, so you run for your bunkers.

So me and Sizemore, was the kid's name, we were running for the bunker, because we were working together that day. And he was slow and I was climbing up his back [laughs] to outrun him. We got to the entrance of the bunker, and the next mortar hit right there at the corner of the bunker, so we got thrown into the bunker. Me and him, we kind of like rolled together all the way down inside the bunker. And the guys were already in it, and they were sitting around. "Oh, hey, guys, glad you could drop in."

The bunkers are set up in an L shape, and, actually, this one had a Z to it. Some hits would hit the wall near the entrance, but the shrapnel and stuff won't go down inside. So that's why you got ninety-degree turns. And this one actually had a Z-shaped entrance to it. But, anyway, it goes down underground, and we just wound up going rolling down into it from the concussion. We each got two or three pieces of shrapnel from it. And that's how I got my purple heart. That's the incident where we got it.

And in that same sequence of those five or six, or whatever it was, rounds that one landed right on one of our eight-inch guns. They had a perimeter around each gun to protect the gunners, but this one hit dead on top of the two guys on the gun. It killed them both. So if you get a direct hit, you're in trouble.

INSIDE OUR PERIMETER

We were up in Khe Sahn, our staging point that we did minesweep from, from Khe Sahn to the Laos border, when these other instances took place with the ARVNs, when I was sitting there when those guys walked up on us. We got hit there one night.

We called them "sappers." They would have satchel chargers. They would try to sneak through the wire wherever they could. They were not suicide bombers, like is used today in the Middle East. They would have these satchel charges full of explosives, and they would try to get inside the perimeter, and then they would run to the bunker entrances, to the ammo dumps, to the helicopters, or whatever there is, and they would pull the pin on these satchels and throw them in. And then they would try to run and get out. So they did not commit suicide, but they would try to get in and blow up everything they can and get back out.

So we got overrun. I think there were twenty-three of them that got in through the wire there one night inside our perimeter. Two of the guys on duty were sleeping. They found the weak spot, and they came in where the guys were sleeping. Of course, they paid the ultimate price for sleeping because they were killed. That's how they got in.

I think we killed most of them. All heck broke loose when everything started blowing up. Then everybody's up, and I, individually, didn't shoot any of them. But the guys got them all. I'm pretty sure our guys got them all, or they think they did. They got in and killed the two of our guys that weren't paying attention. But once everybody woke up, your perimeter triples and quadruples, the people on it, everybody got to their post.

We buried the sappers the next day. Back then, it was nothing like there is today. We just dug a hole, and you push them into it, and you cover them over. That's the way it was in Vietnam. I don't know what they do today in Iraq and Afghanistan when we kill people.

SHIT DUTY

Everybody had their turn at what we'd call "shit burner" of the day. We had outhouses set up with maybe three to five seats in each outhouse. On the back, there's a half of a fifty-five-gallon drum under each toilet seat, and the door would open in the back, and you would slide them out once a day. To dispose of it, rather than digging a hole and burying it, we would burn it. We would pour diesel fuel in it, light it, and then stir it up periodically while it's burning. It wouldn't burn in a big hot flame; it would kind of smolder in the same half a fifty-five-gallon drum. You would just slide it out and keep adding diesel fuel to it and stirring the feces or whatever. Poop. It would take you about six to eight hours to burn it all down to nothing. You would be burning it and stirring it until there would be a little handful of ashes left, about the size of your fist, and that's it.

You would be the one person that would have the four or five or whatever was in that outhouse. You would do them all. That would be your job for the day. You were shit burner of the day.

Once when it was my job for the day, we'd just got up, and we were having breakfast, and the first incoming round of the morning hit the outhouse and blew it up [laughs], so I was put out of a job for the day. It blew shit everywhere. I had to clean it up. I mean it blew the shithouse apart [laughs].

Thinking about that is how I made up that song that I sing to Tommy [McHale], with a cigarette, because he keeps talking about trying to quit. I made up that little poem for him. Let's see:

On top of Ol' Smokey, all covered with shit,
There sat Tommy with a cigarette lit.
He let out a fart, and blew the shithouse apart,
But his cigarette, it stayed lit.

About three months before your duty's up there in Vietnam you fill out what they called a Dream Sheet. If you got more time to do in the service—I had another year and a half—you fill out where you want to go. So everybody talked about the Panama Canal Zone. There was Germany, which was great, but Germany was the cold and the city life. The Canal Zone was the warm tropics and fishing. That was for me.

So I put in for the Canal Zone. When my duty was up in Vietnam, I got my papers for Canal Zone! Yeah! I got it and I had a ball down there. The Canal Zone was definitely the best place for me. I really loved it.

In the Panama Canal Zone, we basically just practiced what we did in Vietnam for real, because probably 50 or 60 percent of the guys there were never in Vietnam. They were just right from the States here and they were excess. They didn't need them in Vietnam, and so they would be stationed in these other places.

But my rank in Panama went back and forth, from private to corporal. I was slated to be a buck sergeant, but I was a little rowdy. I never held my stripes very long. And I would get dissed just for being rowdy—fighting, drinking, coming in late, and stuff like that. But this was all after Vietnam, when I was in the Canal Zone. I got demoted and promoted probably three or four times in my year and a half there.

Probably the biggest instance that had several keys to it was we were sitting in the NCO club drinking, and somebody placed a bet that I couldn't drink six shots of tequila after sitting and drinking rum half the day and night. So I drank the six shots of tequila, but, technically, I couldn't drink them because I was wasted [laughs]. And back then, when you get like that in these places, everything turns into fighting.

So we started fighting in this NCO club. It was air force and army both; we shared it. So we started fighting with the air force guys, and it went outside, and we were drunker than hell. I don't remember exactly how we got broke up.

When I got back to the barracks the sergeant that was the night duty officer, CQ they called them, said something that upset me. I was already upset, I guess, so I started fighting with him. That was one instance of my demotion [laughs]. I got promoted again, but for me, Panama was a party [laughs]. I got paid to party. I was in Panama about a year and a half and Vietnam a year. It was a three-year stint all together.

I did some fishing in Vietnam with hand grenades. We'd get up in the mountain areas in these creeks, mainly. Just to eat something different or just want to see what kind of fish are in there, because I'm a fishing enthusiast, I'd take a hand grenade and throw it in and see what floats up. And every place we ever did it, it wasn't always me that did it, but when I was with anybody that ever did it, we always got the same fish. It was always one kind of fish that kind of looked like a tilapia, after seeing a tilapia here. I mean sometimes there'd be fifty of them would float up. We'd eat them. But we never saw another kind of fish. That was the only kind of fish we ever saw in the areas where we were. Now, this was the mountainous, hilly rain forest country. But that was always the same kind of fish.

When I got down near the ocean, there it's a different story. We'd catch red snapper, kingfish, and grouper. This was fishing. We'd go down to the docks where the locals were, the Vietnamese, and they used hand-lines—basically what we do except it was Dacron hand-lines. It wasn't even clear stuff. And they would go out there with their hooks and catch their snapper, grouper, whatever, in the South China Sea. It was very crude stuff, so I could imagine if you went over there with some good monofilament leaders and stuff like we use, you could really catch 'em.

I never went out in the boats with them. I just went down to where they fished. It wasn't really much of a dock. They'd pull the fish up on the beach. There were some little rivers, with a village just inside with an opening like we would call an inlet. Of course, they didn't have any rocks or jetties to make it an official inlet. But there were places where our military ships went in, cargo ships, where we built docks. I believe it was Cam Ranh Bay where we actually had ships come there.

LEGAL TROUBLE IN NORTH CAROLINA

A couple of my other buddies, from when we were in the Canal Zone, we all got out at the same time. One lived in Tampa, one lived in Miami, one lived in Georgia, and one lived in North Carolina, and we all got together. We were in North Carolina and we were drinking.

They've got dry counties and wet counties up there. And the police, of course, would wait right across the line of a wet county, and when you come into the dry county at twelve or one o'clock in the morning, they did the alcohol test.

And we come across from partying, coming around the side of this mountain, and I was flying. I had a '73 Barracuda back then, and we were coming down around this mountain. I was going a little bit too fast, and we were too drunk. So I realized it was a pretty sharp curve ahead and, of course, I hit the brakes hard and went into a spin. We spun right around the curve, luckily, and stopped with the front of the car looking right over a 500-foot cliff. And we didn't say a word. I just backed down and we went on down the road.

Just about a mile across the county line, cops had the thing set up. So they pulled us over and made me get out. Of course, I was intoxicated. My buddies were intoxicated worse than I was, but they put me in the car and take me to the station, and they have my buddies drive the car. They were just as drunk as I was. Funny. But they didn't say anything to them. They followed me down to the police station. They take me in there, where they had a kangaroo court set up. They actually had a judge and everything there in the middle of the night.

I was out of the service, and this was a month or so after we got out. So the judge says, "Mr. Kaul, your alcohol level is such-and-such." They had the little blue thing set up there to test your alcohol, and I was well past the legal limit. "How do you plead?"

And I said, "Guilty."

"Uhm," he said. "Well, that'll be $198 fine or ten days in jail."

I said, "Well, I'll have to take the ten days." So he paused for a minute. I said, "I don't have that much money."

So he fumbles around for a little bit. And he says, "Well, how about if I lower the fine to a hundred dollars?"

They just wanted the money. They didn't want me to sit ten days in jail. That's what this is all about. So he says, "A hundred dollars or ten days in jail."

I says, "Well, I'll take the ten days, your Honor, because I don't have a hundred dollars."

So he stopped because I didn't have the hundred dollars. So he says, "Uh, Mr. Kaul, how much money *do* you have?"

I said, "$44."

He said, "Okay, the fine's $44, or ten days in jail."

I says, "Ah, I'll still have to take the ten days in jail."

He started steaming then. He says, "What's wrong now?"

I says, "Well, I'm in North Carolina. I'm eight hundred miles from Florida," I says. "This is all the money I got." Back then, you didn't have credit cards or nothing. I says, "I need at least enough money for gas and at least one meal to get back to Florida."

So he says, "Okay, Mr. Kaul, how much money do you need to get back to Florida?"

I said, "Well, at least twenty bucks." You know, back then, gas was cheap and stuff. "So at least, I'd say, twenty bucks."

He said, "Okay, your fine's $22" [laughs].

Okay, settled. So I got up and I, oh, had a victory! I started to walk, and he said, "Oh, no, no, no. You can't leave yet. You have to stay here in jail for at least six hours after being arrested."

So they got me for six hours. I sat there for six hours. And my buddies came and got me, but it was funny. I mean, all they wanted was the money, whatever they could get out of you. They didn't want to keep you around for ten days [laughs].

COMMERCIAL FISHING

I never went back to college. I bought me an 18-foot Sun Coast and started doing a little net fishing. My brother was a teenager then, and I was probably twenty-three. My brother is seven years younger, and he had a little net boat. He was fishing with Dale Jackson, Terry Cheetum, and a couple of other guys. They were buddies and were net fishing in the river.

So I got an 18-foot Sun Coast and I started doing it, too. I was spot fishing, trout fishing, and stuff in the river. I did that for a while, and then one day Nick Kurusis asked me if I wanted to fish his boat. So I fished his boat, and I would kingfish with my father in between.

We would go out on the *Aurora*, which he had built up. At this time my father was commercial fishing, but not for a living. It was just for fun, because you didn't need licenses. There were no requirements. So rather than go out and catch sailfish and throw them back, we went out, caught kingfish, and we would sell them. It would pay for our fishing.

So Nick asked me if I wanted to fish his kingfish boat. So I said, "Sure, yeah." So Nick and I started fishing. I would take the boat some;

Nick would go with me some. But we fished, and Nick and I fished good together. We worked out good together. We caught a lot of fish. We had a couple thousand pounds one day, which was, individually, the biggest catch that either one of us had ever had. It was around a couple thousand pounds. And Nick and I fished together like that for, I'd say, about a year and a half.

And then I bought a Luhrs boat from Chuck Davis. He let me make payments on it, through the fish house, because B. C. Davis was running the co-op at the time. That was the kingfishermen's co-op, and I made payments through there. They took out about 20 percent every week and paid Chuck for the boat. I had the boat paid off pretty quick and had that boat for two or three years.

Then Herman Summerlin had the *Big Chief.* The boat was in Herman Summerlin's name when I bought it. Chief [Anselmo Santes] was quitting fishing for whatever reason at the time and wanted to sell it or give it back to Herman, because it was in Herman's name. But I bought the *Big Chief* from Herman. It was October of '77. And of course, it was for kingfishing first, and then swordfishing came later, after Martin Styer and Billy Minuth and I teamed up together on the *Little Bits* and started swordfishing.

THE BIG CHIEF

In 1971 the *Big Chief* was washed up on the beach. It was a drug-smuggling boat that was stolen from somebody. Whoever the drug people were, they didn't get caught. But they run the boat on the beach, dumped the drugs off, and just left the boat. All that marijuana residue was in the boat, even when I had it, three or four years later. If I got down inside along the gunnels and stringers down in there, there was marijuana seeds and stuff still in there. They probably weren't any good anymore, but you could still see the seeds.

Then, while it was on the beach, somebody come and cut the side out of it, unbolted the motors, and tried to drag them out and up the beach. They got them halfway up the beach. I believe they were Perkins diesels. They got them halfway up the beach and quit.

Herman's oldest boy, Roy, went down there and pulled guard on the boat after this had happened. So the guys didn't get the motors, because it got sunlight and they left them. But then the next day, they pulled

George landing king mackerel on the *Big Chief*.

guard and were watching it so they didn't get them. Whoever was trying to steal them came close to getting them. They were just too heavy to get across that soft sand and get up the beach in one night.

The *Big Chief* was salvaged. And then Chief fixed it up and king-fished in it. I don't know if it was still in Herman's name or Chief's name when Chief was fishing it, but when I bought it, I bought it from Herman. Those motors were taken out, and Chief put a single 3160 Caterpillar. And that motor was still in it for the first ten years that I had it. I've put two new Caterpillars in it since owning it. The 25-foot Luhrs that I got from B. C. Davis actually was my own first kingfish boat.

FIRST YEARS

I used to keep a log. I kept a log on everything. That's one thing I always did. I was pretty good at keeping numbers. Like I say, in school I was good with numbers, math, but English, forget it, literature, that stuff. I kept a log on my daily catches and totals at the end of the year. In my first years, I don't remember the number of years, but according to my books, my average catch was 920 pounds a day, winter and summer. That's what I averaged per day. That was starting in the '70s to the early '80s.

Now, when the fish stock started going down, of course, these numbers were going down, too. I don't remember the year, exactly, they started going down, but as I kept my logs, you could see them, first couple years was 920 pounds a day. Then it would get to 800 and something, then 700 and some, then 600 and then 500. The last year I kept a log, it was in the later '90s, it got down to the average was 125 pounds a day for the year. Then I just quit keeping a log [laughs].

But for twenty years or more, I kept that. And it started out, the winter catches would be 1,500 to 1,800 pounds on the real good days. The average days would be 800 to 1,000, or 1,100 or 1,200. In the summertime, I would say the average catches were 300 to 600. And a lot more if there was good days. We had weeks in August and May, they were the big summer months, where we'd catch 1,000 to 1,300 pounds. Augusts and Mays, back then, were really good. So for the year, the average was big.

SWORDFISHING

As the stocks of fish went down, swordfishing came into this area. I believe Billy Minuth was the first one to go out and set a swordfish line here. He set a short piece of line here, and I think they caught three fish on a short piece of line the first time he went out.

Swordfish lines are like trout lines. You'd have a half-mile of line with, maybe, thirty hooks on it. You'd put a buoy maybe every 500 feet to support it and that the fish would fight against. And you let it drift with the Gulf Stream. I don't know how long Billy set that first line; he let it drift. But we would set them at first dark and pick them up at daylight. Traditionally, that's what you would do.

I got into it with Billy and Martin Styer on the *Little Bits*, Martin Styer's boat. In 1978 the three of us went in a partnership. We split the costs and everything three ways. We did not catch a whole lot of fish to start with.

Leland Curry and my brother, who was fishing with Leland, they were catching good fish. I finally cornered my brother one day and I said, "David," I says, "y'all are catching ten times more than we are. We catch, you know, 2-, 300 pounds, and y'all are catching 2,000 pounds a night." I says, "What are we doing wrong?"

My brother finally told me. Leland was trying to keep it a secret. The people that were doing it, that were getting the big catches, were using light sticks, Calumet light sticks. So my brother finally told me. We got the light sticks, and, immediately, we're averaging the same weight as them.

Plastic light sticks. The Calumet light sticks had two chemicals in it. You got a rubber soft outer cylinder with one chemical and then you got a little plastic cylinder inside that, or a thin glass cylinder inside that, with another chemical in it. And you bend it and break the inside cylinder, and the two chemicals flow together, and they cause a glow for approximately ten hours, and then the light dies.

You would put one about six to eight feet above each hook, and that made all the difference in the world. That light down there in the dark water at night would attract squid and bait and stuff to it, and then also the swordfish would come along, and they'd start to feed. They'd get the Boston mackerel that you had hanging on your hook or the squid or whatever you used. Our production went up dramatically.

So my brother let the cat out of the bag to us there, and then he jumped ship and came fishing with me the next year, because I started using my own boat. And I only fished the one year with Martin and Billy. Then I started using the *Big Chief* the next year, and my brother and Brant Mc-Manus started fishing with me. The three of us fished a couple of years. Brant probably fished three years with me. My brother fished two, and then he went off to college. He continued on with his college education.

I was a fisherman, not a scholar. I got more into swordfishing because of the depletion in the winter stocks of kingfishing, and the money was much bigger in the swordfishing at this time than it was in the kingfishing.

NEW ENGLAND SWORDFISHING

Up in the New England area they had been swordfishing for years before this. One of the main methods there for catching swordfish was the harpoon. They had harpoon boats, and then they used this longlining method. Today's show, *Swords*, on Discovery, shows you basically that they've been doing that for many, many years up in that area.

It just migrated down to learning that the swords were down in this area, too. They followed the Gulf Stream, and they had to come through the Straits of Florida to wind up up there. Because they would circle with the Gulf Stream, and it was only in '77 that the first boat or two came down this way to try it, and it worked. So that started a new fishery in this area, and it was banner for years. They still do it here, but today the government, with the Bahamas, shut the Straits off, so we can't fish out here in front anymore.

Now you have to go to the Northeast and get out of that 200-mile radius. That's where they fish today. But the fishing is basically still the same principle, just got to go further and need a bigger boat. The catches did go down here in this area, because there was so many fishing.

It was such a lucrative thing for a while. Like anything, when it's good, everybody wants to get into it. It doesn't matter what business it is; if somebody's doing really good and making big money, it's not long before there's other people venturing into the same business.

So, yes, we had too many boats here for a while, and it was hard to find a place to put your line out. Gradually, as the lines got longer and the more boats there were, it was harder to get a decent catch. There was so many boats filling in all the spots in between that it cut down the catch on everybody. Those that weren't doing very well got out, and then there were a lot fewer boats left.

I was one that got out and went back to kingfishing. Some of the bigger boats stayed because they could go out a little further, spread out more gear, and still make a good living at it.

Well, Billy's experimental line was only about a half a mile. When we went to actually fishing, we started with three miles that first year. I'd say when most of us got going, we started with about three miles. Then we'd quickly go to five or six miles. And in the three years that I did it, I started with three and I ended up with twelve miles of line on the *Big Chief*. I had twelve miles at the end of my third year.

I actually did it four years, but the fourth year was only for a short period. Brant McManus or my brother weren't with me any longer. I had hired some other people, and the catches were small for a month or two in my fourth year there, and I wasn't making much, so I quit.

Overhead wasn't bad back then. Five, six hundred dollars was all it was for a trip. Today, it's a bit different, because back then fuel was fifty-six cents a gallon. You didn't get charged for ice. The bait, the Boston mackerel we used, if I remember right, it was only thirty or forty cents a pound, so you could go fishing. The light sticks were your biggest expense; they were a buck apiece.

In the beginning, for every three miles, we would use twenty hooks, 20-foot leaders, and we would put a hook about every hundred feet. As we got on into it, we learned to go to longer leaders. We went to 40-foot leaders and then to 80-foot leaders. Then, my last year, it was 120-foot leaders, and the longer you made your leaders, the less hooks you would put out. So on the twelve miles at the end, the leaders were 120 foot. On the twelve miles a hundred hooks, probably, is all there was, a hundred light sticks and hooks.

SHARK FISHING

After I quit swordfishing, probably about '82, shark fishing was just coming around. So Brant McManus and I and, later, George Johnson decided to start shark fishing. We heard selling the fins would be profitable.

We used the same principle as swordfishing, only with real short leaders and 550-pound mono. We'd put a short piece of cable on it, with the hook, so the teeth wouldn't cut through. And we went out there with a short piece—I don't remember exactly, maybe a half a mile or whatever it was in length. But we'd put a hook every four or five foot with a short leader. Maybe it was 6 hooks every twenty feet on the line. I think we put 125 hooks on it, whatever the length that we had. And at first, with 125 hooks, we probably had 120 sharks. I mean, it was unbelievable.

So then we had to clean them and dress them and cut the heads off. We had sharp knives and stuff. The bigger sharks took longer, but you'd get used to it. You zip the fins off and throw them aside. Back then when we were doing it, there was no money for the fins yet. We didn't even keep the fins. We were just catching them to sell the meat. That's all we were doing. It was just strictly meat. We decided it was too much work to mess with the fins. About a year or so after we quit, that's when the fin market came. We were not getting anything for fins, just the meat.

And we cut off several sharks that were just too big to handle. I mean, we just didn't want to try to put them in the boat. Big bull sharks and tiger sharks, monster things that we just cut off. We did put one big bull shark in the boat, which was a pretty good-size shark, probably 300 pounds cleaned in the hold. When you dress him out, the meat size is a hundred and some pounds, after you cut everything off.

We had one that had no food in his stomach, but he had a Texas license plate, a two-by-four about twenty inches long, and he had about a third of a street tire. Now, he obviously didn't bite the tire, but it was about a third piece of a tire in his stomach, and that was it. There was no food whatsoever. Of course, they say fish, when they get stressed and get on the hook, they regurgitate all the food out, and obviously he couldn't with the license plate and the tire and the two-by-four. No telling how long they were in his stomach. The license plate was perfectly clean and legible, but it was a Texas license plate. I don't know if that shark had swallowed that license plate in Texas or here, but it was a long ways from Texas.

BIG SEA

Brant McManus and I were swordfishing. We went alone that particular day. It was supposed to be 10 to 15 out of the northeast, which, if that's what it was, it would have been fine. We get out there and things changed. We ran down between Jupiter and Palm Beach. We ran halfway across, roughly to the middle, what we call the Straits, halfway across, between Florida and the Bahamas. We were probably out about thirty miles when we set our gear.

That night I think I set all twelve miles. So we started this side of the centerline and went over the centerline, roughly five miles, six miles, or whatever, on each side when we got all the gear out. There was a little breeze. It was nothing bad, but during the night in the darkness we noticed a change.

Of course, we were on the east end of the line at this time. The swells were getting bigger and bigger. We were on the east side of our gear, which was east of the main current of the flow of the Gulf Stream, where it's going to the north. We were on the other side of the current. But our west end of our gear was right in the heart of the current. So we had a gentle swell at daylight of probably about fifteen foot when we woke up. I mean, and then we could really see, but it was far apart, which wasn't bad. So we start picking up our gear, and we come to this one fish.

Our drift all depends on how hard the Gulf Stream is flowing on that particular night. It varies anywheres from as much as 5 knots down to, sometimes, almost a dead stop. That night we had about a 2½-knot drift, and from where we were, because it took us a long time to get our gear in, I mean, we come in from a little north of east of Fort Pierce, so it was not a hard drift. But we covered probably sixty miles from south to north.

We started picking up the gear, and we came to this one big fish—a big fish. The fish dressed out at about 360 pounds. So it was a thousand-dollar fish for the night. It was just Brant and me, and it's borderline trying to fish with just two people. The fish probably was 500 pounds whole, before you dress him.

The two of us trying to get that fish in the boat under normal conditions would be tough to begin with. Here the boat is surging with fifteen-foot waves, swells, but every time we would get the fish to the boat, get a hook in and try to board it, a swell would come and toss the boat, and you just could not hang onto the fish. It was just too much. And we would have to let him go, let the spool free-spool, so we don't tear him off. Then we get him to the boat again, try to time it and get him in the boat.

We tried for an hour and could not get the timing right with the waves to get him in the boat without a wave picking us up and surging us. We had a tuna door in the stern, so we'd get him there, and all we had to do was get him up about eight inches to slide him in. But the two of us, with that weight, because the fish was so big and the sea surging, we just weren't strong enough to do it. Mother Nature was putting too much against us. Under normal conditions, we probably would have been able to do it easily.

Finally, I said to Brant, "Look, we're killing ourselves here. And we're not getting anywhere. We've been an hour on this fish, and we're not getting it in. Let's just cut him off and go."

Brant didn't want to do that. He didn't want to give up and says, "Let's try one more time."

So we did it one more time, and we got it in the boat, and the next wave—the boat, I think, had turned to where the stern was into the wave as it came—and as it started to surge, it lifts the fish up. Then because the boat was flat-sterned to it, it kind of built up a wall of water there and it kind of washed the fish right into the boat [laughs]. I mean, it was like we didn't hardly have to pull that time; it just washed him right in. But we were wore out after that. I mean, just an hour trying to get that fish into the boat, back and forth with those big waves, trying to get him. That wave washed him in the boat, so that solved that.

We continued getting our gear in, and then we started getting further to the west in the heart of that Gulf Stream. It was like the outgoing tide in the inlet. The waves got bigger and closer together and were breaking. We were looking at each other and the size of them waves breaking over us, just like you see in the Bering Sea with the crab guys [*Deadliest Catch*]. I mean, those waves were just covering us.

But the *Big Chief* took it. I mean, it took it good. I had the deck sealed. We had the tuna door opened. Every time a big wall of water come in the boat, it could go out that big tuna door, and everything was sealed up into the cockpit. For the size of the boat, we fared good. And we finally got everything in and started in.

LOST BOAT

That same trip, Gene Hayes, Bobby Christensen, and Raymond Hassel-grove's boat, the *Going Broke*, were out on that same trip. Don (I don't remember Don's last name) was running Raymond Hasselgrove's boat. Gene Hayes got his gear in first and was going on home way ahead of us. But Bobby C. and me and Don on the *Going Broke* all finished about the same time. We're all heading to the west, and I mean it was brutal. It was really nasty for our size boats.

My boat was 32 feet, Bobby C.'s boat was 39, and the *Going Broke*, Don's boat, was 42 foot, so he had the biggest boat. He had side ex-hausts in the back, not out the stern, but on the side, and where it was glassed through with all the twisting and stuff, somewhere in that weather those exhausts broke loose. That's what we figured happened. Water, not only from the exhaust of the motor running, but ocean wa-ter, was all coming into the boat. The boat was getting stern-heavy as more and more water was accumulating. Pretty soon the boat was not rising with the waves, because it was getting so heavy with water.

Don started to notice that, and he slowed down. Of course, when you're up trying to run, and then you got this big buildup of water, but the amount of water in there has gotten so far ahead of you, the weight is tremendous from the water. Then when you slow down, all the water runs forward and the boat just kind of nosedives into the next wave. So then the water's just coming all over the side and everything, because there's just so much water in the boat, the bow's not rising; it's just washing over it.

He immediately got on the radio and said that he was in trouble. The boat was full of water, and I think the motors died, too, when the water ran forward. And the next transmission was that they were going to get in the fish box and he gave his position.

Bobby C. was the closest and got over to him and told us he got him. He picked them up and they were okay. Nobody lost their lives. They got in the fish box. Everybody got picked up, but the boat went quick once the water had been building up in there from where them exhausts had broke loose.

So that's the way I remember it. I could be a little bit off on exactly the sequence, but they got picked up, and we headed home.

Once we got out of the Gulf Stream and started to get to the kingfish grounds in eighty-five feet there, seventy-five feet, the waves weren't a foot and a half high [laughs]. It was unbelievable the difference out there in the Stream to in here. It was a situation where the weather forecast, initially, was suitable for us to go. And during the night, the weather intensified, and of course, they changed their weather forecast at midnight or something.

We already had all this gear in the water, and there was nothing we could do, so we just had to ride with it. And by daylight it was 25 knots northeast, and in the middle of the Stream, it was a good twenty foot. That was the worst, individually, for any period like that.

STORMS

Now, I've been caught in thunderstorms for twenty, thirty minutes, where it blows really hard. Matter of fact, on another swordfishing trip, it was probably early in the season, when the cold fronts were still coming through, I got caught in the squall line, where the front first comes through, and you get your initial blast of 60- to 80-mile-an-hour winds, sometimes for five minutes or so when it first hits.

I was east of Bethel [Shoals], and that hit. And I mean, it blew whatever, 60 to 80—I don't know what it blew. And the waves got up to where they were only about three to four feet apart. But they were six- to seven-foot high. It was unbelievable.

And the shock on the boat from these waves being so close, hitting the boat, caused my bulkhead to crack. I had two or three other cracks in the cabin just from the shock of it happening. It was because of the hardness of the water hitting the boat, and there was no rise and fall of the boat, because the waves were so close together. Two or three waves were on the boat at all times, from stem to stern, and it cracked the boat in about three places. Luckily, it only lasted a few minutes. But those waves built to straight up and down as hard as the wind blew.

And then the wind dropped out, and the waves spread out and leveled back out. It didn't last long, but it just shows you how quick and how rough the water can get when the wind reaches a certain intensity. When the wind's against the current, it's like the outgoing tide of the inlet.

LIGHTNING

When Martin Styer and Billy Minuth and I were in our first year swordfishing, we were in a lightning storm there one night, from right after we set our gear till four in the morning, for about six hours. We seemed to drift with this lightning storm to the north, and lightning was popping all around the boat, all night long. You had to just cover your eyes. You couldn't keep your eyes even open, that's how bad it was. It seemed like a thousand bolts hit within a few feet of the boat. Bolts of lightning hit within a few hundred feet of the boat. It was unbelievable. None ever hit the boat, but it was blinding and deafening.

WATERSPOUT

Ah, might have been one of those days, when Loretta was with me, off of Jupiter. We were fishing in Jupiter, middle of the day. We would go anchor up, and I would stay on the boat overnight. And Loretta and I anchored the boat up. And it was around twelve o'clock noon, and a storm was coming, and I said, "Well, let's go down and take a nap, go to sleep and let the storm blow over."

So we went down there, and lying down in the bunk, all of a sudden it sounded like a freight train was going over the boat. It was a roar like you'd never heard before. And then the boat starts tilting over, and this roar, and I realized then what it was. It was a waterspout just came right down over the boat. It sounded like a freight train running over you, and the boat actually leaned over about thirty degrees. It was intense for a few seconds, but that's all it was.

JUPITER, FLORIDA

In Jupiter you would go and unload, or you would anchor up. And sometimes I'd put out a bottom-fishing line and do a little bottom-fishing in between. Well, Loretta got her biggest kingfish in Jupiter.

Might have been the same trip the waterspout hit us; I don't remember. Got the picture here of her with it.

I was talking on the radio, as I am prone to do [laughs], and Loretta's back there yelling at me. She was jerking the bug. That fish was caught on the bug, and she was a hollerin' she had a whale, something was about to pull her out of the boat. And I was talking on the radio.

She said, "You better get back here and help me!" [laughs].

So, finally, I put the mike down, and I went back there, and that's when we ended up with a forty-four-pound kingfish for her.

Loretta with a forty-four-pound kingfish caught in Jupiter, Florida.

I caught a seventy-two-pound wahoo when I was home on leave from the service on the *Lou Donna* in 1971, the boat my father had for about a year and a half. We were out there northeast of the inlet; I don't remember the exact location. Back then we had the LORAN A was all. But we were northeast of the inlet there in roughly sixty-five feet of water, and we were just trolling to the north.

All of the sudden—we were pretty new at kingfishing—we'd only been learning it the last two, three years. I was on a thirty-day leave from the service, and we got this big fish on. And I remember I said to my father, "It's a big kingfish."

So my father said to me, "Well, put it in the boat!" [laughs].

So after I gaffed it and put it in the boat, it turns out it's a big wahoo. It was a seventy-two-pound wahoo. I just pulled him right in. Nothing dramatic there.

Today, I would have gone all nervous, pulling that fish up to the back of the boat. I'd been shaking and everything. But back then I was young and strong and not anticipating something like that. Now you get a big fish on, you know it's a really big kingfish or wahoo, so you get kind of tense about it. But back then it was kind of new, and I never even thought of a fish that size.

BIGGEST KINGFISH

But then, my biggest kingfish was fifty-one pounds. I caught that on the Northeast Grounds in July on the outrigger, on a sea witch. Oh, yeah, I gaffed him. Big fish like that I gaff. Twenty-five pounds and up, I gaff; twenty pounds and under, I don't. And then in between there, it depends. Usually, once they get up into twenty pounds or better, I gaff everything anymore. It was a fifty-one-pound kingfish.

BIG COBIAS

It was only about five or six years ago I caught one of my biggest cobias. I had, within two weeks, I caught a fifty-five- and a forty-five-pound cobia. The fifty-fiver was north of 12A Buoy, and the forty-five was on the offshore bar straight east of north of 12A. They were about two weeks apart. That was my two biggest cobias.

BIGGEST SWORDFISH

And then Billy Minuth and Martin Styer and I caught the biggest sword-fish that I was ever connected with. It dressed out at 513 pounds. That was Billy, Martin, and I. But we had a block and tackle on the side of the boat, and it took us an hour to get it in the boat. But it dressed out at 513.

ODD HAPPENING

I come in from fishing and went home one day. I come back down the next morning to go fishing and got down to the boat, and the boat's running [laughs]. It's ready to go. I guess I forgot to shut it off when I walked off it the day before. It was still sitting there idling [laughs].

FREAK WAVES

I was going out one July, and this was only three or four years ago, and I was there about the Hurricane Rock. And like I said, it was July; it was slick calm. And all of a sudden, ahead of me I could see this wall of water breaking. It was, like, 300 feet wide. That's all it was. And I sat there looking at it, like, shit, it's getting closer. I quickly closed my window, because a summertime morning, you got your window open. I quickly closed my window, and it was about a 10-foot-high wave, just breaking. And there were two waves. There was that one, and then the one behind, it was maybe 7 foot. And then that was it. It was back to a slick calm ocean again. But it was just two big waves in the middle of a calm ocean.

I've seen where all of a sudden, one wave in the middle of a rough situation is, like, two times or more bigger than all the rest of them, but not a situation where the ocean is basically almost flat, and all of a sudden, a big wave like it covered the whole ocean. It was at least 300 foot wide and 10 foot high, the first one. The next one was about 7 foot.

WAYWARD BOAT

My little net boat, not the *Big Chief*, but my 18-foot Sun Coast, I come down in the morning to go fishing, and my boat wasn't there. So as it started to get daylight, I don't remember now who it was, we went out and looked around. We rode out in the river and saw it all the way across the river, on the east side of the river, laying up against the mangroves. We saw a boat and figured, well, that must be it. And we went over there, and, sure enough, that was it. I guess I didn't tie it up, and it just got off.

Now, I've done that numerous times with the *Big Chief*, where you don't put all the ropes on. And I come down the next morning and there's only one rope or two ropes holding it, where normally I'd have a couple, a spring line, a couple on the bow, a couple on the stern. And I'd only have one or two of them on. I've done that and didn't put all the ropes on. But this day I guess I walked off and didn't put any on. I guess it floated out of the marina and across the river.

LONG HOURS

Back then, in the '70s there, I was not married. And I fished daylight to dark. And I'd go out and party till twelve or one o'clock in the morning. Of course, I was in my twenties then. I was young, and I would go out and party all night, till one in the morning, two in the morning. Come right back the next day, go back fishing. It never bothered you. Fished till dark.

Today, of course, with quotas, and me, individually, being much older, physically, I couldn't stay and fish till dark. Nor, with the quotas, in most situations you're going to have your quota met if there's any amount of fish around long before dark. The quotas are small today compared to the days I'm talking about. In the '70s, we'd catch fifteen, sixteen, seventeen, eighteen hundred pounds on the good days. And the average days would be six [hundred] to a thousand. Six hundred to a thousand would be your average days in the wintertime back then. You'd have some poor days. There was always some poor days, even back then.

But, basically, youth and more fish made a big difference back then in the overall fishery production. So if you had the physical stamina and the youth and you'd put the time in, you're going to catch a lot of fish back in those days. Today, there's more restrictions on your fishing, and I don't think there's as many fish today as there used to be years ago. There are times in the winter and during certain times of the year when there is some good runs. If you did stay and you weren't on limits, I think you still could catch fifteen hundred to eighteen hundred pounds on certain days. But with the limits and stuff today, you don't get the opportunity.

What prompted my wife, Loretta, to quit staying on the boat with me in Jupiter [laughs]? Well, I guess the story about that little waterspout probably had a little bit to do with it, but I think more so was the night adventures on the boat. Meaning, we had friends on the boat—a lot of friends, some nights.

Ah, this one particular night we settled down and put the lights out, and all of a sudden, Loretta says . . . I never paid no attention to it because I lived with them all the time, so I just ignored them . . . and Loretta says, "What's all that little crawling, rustling sound?"

And I say, "What?"

She says, "Don't you hear it? All that little racket, like there's something scraping or crawling on the walls or something?"

I said, "Oh, that's just a few roaches. Don't worry about them."

So she says, "It's got to be more than a few to make that much noise." So she said, "Turn on a light."

So I had to get up, turn on the light, and when she saw [laughs] thousands of roaches, all scurrying, she wouldn't sleep in the cabin anymore. She went out in the cockpit, the deck area. And she never spent the night on the boat again. That was the end of it. She didn't like sleeping with my bug friends.

KINGFISHING

Kingfishing has been good for me. I always wanted to be a fisherman. Fishing's what I've done most of my life. I decided to be a fisherman when I couldn't hack the school stuff. People always ask me why'd I want to become a fisherman, and I said, "Well, because I was too stupid to do anything else, and you didn't need any brains to be a fisherman" [laughs]. So that's why I became a fisherman.

When I first got out of the service and first started kingfishing, I became good friends with Elmer Stokes. He used to say, in a joking way, "Kingfishing was a lazy man's fishing." That's what he always called it, because you just sit there, and you put your line on, and you wait for a bite. On slow days, of course, it's relaxing, and so he always joked about it, that it was the lazy man's fishing.

Now anybody that is real competitive at it and tries to be top dog knows you have to work your butt off in order to be in the top fish line in any fishing business. It's not really a lazy man's fishing; it's a lot of work. To fight Mother Nature alone is tough, much less the actual fishing. You're out there all the time, and you're getting all these weather situations.

JERK-BUG FISHING

Roger Farlow and I become real good friends. In the '80s we did a lot of things together. We'd talk about jerk-bug fishing. He was an expert bug fisherman. I always used to put bait on a bug, and he'd laugh at me, and he'd say to me, "Why do you put bait on your bug?"

"Because I can't get a bite if I don't!" [laughs].

And he'd just laugh and say, "George, you don't need bait." That was his favorite thing to say. Then he'd say, "Put the bug out there and jerk it. Just keep jerking it until you start catching fish on it. Once you get the hang of it, of the rhythm of the jerk, and you start catching, you'll never put a piece of bait on a bug again."

Finally, I started doing it, and I never put a piece of bait on a bug again. And he was right. You don't need bait on a jerk bug. You just got to get over that psychological thing that's all in your head. If you got it in your mind that what you're fishing with and how you're doing it just isn't going to work, your heart's not in it, so you're not doing the right motion or speed that you need to be doing. Once you get over that and you learn the correct methods and do it correctly, it's going to work. I never put another thing on a bug. Roger broke me of that. I'll give Roger lots of credit for that.

George with an eight-pound bass caught in his pond behind his house.

He turned me into a bass fisherman, too, and Roger and I spent a lot of time together. I wish, in the later years, I'd spent a little more time with him. But in the '80s and early '90s, we did a lot together.

ROGER'S FIRE

Roger Farlow, one of my best friends over the years, had a fire aboard his boat. I wasn't fishing on the day it happened. He was close to five miles out and on his way in when he noticed smoke coming up from his engine box. His motor started to gasp first, and he looked back and noticed there was a little smoke coming up around the engine box. He opened his engine box and saw that his fuel line had been cut by a short in the wire that ran across the fuel line (this is what he figures happened). It ignited the fuel, and when he opened the engine box and the air got to it, she really blazed up. He only had enough time to get on the radio and say that he was on fire. And he had to get out of the boat because the fire was so hot.

The other boats saw the smoke, and Jimmy Ryan, who also was a hand-line fisherman like the rest of us and had one of the faster boats, ran right in there and picked Roger up after John Giorodono, a recreational fisherman, had reached Roger first and pulled him out of the water. Roger's boat burned to the water and sank. Roger lost the whole boat. That was Roger's dream boat, the *Sumaran*. He had built that boat up from scratch. It was the boat he always wanted.

GROUPER FISHING

He [Roger] taught me how to bottom-fish, and we caught a lot of grouper together. Before that, I didn't know anything about it. We fished with hand-lines. Roger taught me the basic method that we used, which was to use a 200-pound test main line with a three-way swivel on it and put your lead about a foot off the bottom end of the three-way, about a foot down. Then use 150-pound test hook leader, depending on how much tide you have. The more tide, the longer you make your hook leader, and the less tide, the shorter you make your leader. So if you have no tide, you can fish seven or eight feet. When you have more tide you want to lengthen that leader out to somewhere around eighteen to twenty feet. When there's a fair amount of tide, the lead would be a foot below the swivel. For bait we liked a half a pogie. You slice or cut a pogie at a forty-five-degree angle and hook him through the head and then let him flutter back there.

FORT PIERCE PORPOISE

Everybody knows that porpoise feed on the kingfish. When the porpoise see the commercial kingfish boats come out in the morning, they've got in the habit of running up to us. You can see them tailing the water and come up to your boat. And sometimes they'd do a flip, like they're so glad to see you. Then they get behind your boat, wait for you to get a kingfish on, and then they take it. So they're glad to see you, but you're not glad to see them.

Well, this one particular day, I was just sitting there. It was a relatively calm day, and I just happened to look out ahead of the boat, and there's a porpoise sitting up on his tail, just looking at the boat. He was just stationary in the water, sitting on his tail, two-thirds of his body out of the water. He was just holding himself there like they do at Marineland. He was sitting up on his tail, standing up on his tail and looking left and right, just looking at the boats. You could see him moving his head, just observing. And then finally he decides where he's going to go, right? Well, I guess he was picking out a boat.

It's kind of unbelievable maybe, but they're just inquisitive and observant of what's going on. I don't remember now if it was the same day or a couple days later that Mike MacManus called me and said he just saw the porpoise doing exactly the same thing, standing up on his tail, looking, and just holding itself out of the water and looking at the boats, as if he's trying to pick out who he's going to go to. I thought that was quite unique. It was fairly close to the same time that he saw exactly the same thing.

Sometimes you'll see all of them when they're following behind your boat, and all of a sudden, the porpoise either come up and get a gulp or make a lunge forward and go down. And you'll see the change in his speed and what he's doing, and you'll know, "Oh, I'm going to get a bite." And you just wait to see which outrigger is going to come up. And sure enough, the outrigger comes up, and you get a bite. I don't know what it is, their sonar or they see the fish coming or they sense it, but they know before you get a bite that you're going to get one.

I think this porpoise problem originated in the '50s in Hobe Sound. As time went on and they have their young, their mothers train their young. We see it here in the last twenty years. The mothers will have their young alongside them, and they bring them up, and you'll see the first couple of times, it'll be like there's a small porpoise pulling on your line, and you can pull it away. But they only let you get it so far, then the mother grabs it and just—ugh!—like a truck, and rips it all off. So you can see the mother is training the young.

Over a period of time, the population keeps growing as these young mature. Then they have their young, and they train their young. It started in Hobe Sound. They never used to be up here in Fort Pierce until it started in about the middle '80s. And it used to be only on the south end offshore, the very south end of the Fort Pierce Grounds.

Tommy McHale used to say the porpoise were taking his fish, and I never would believe it, because I never liked to fish the south end. I would fish east of the inlet up to the Northeast Grounds. That was my primary area for fishing, and I just didn't believe Tommy. I used to call him out at the dock about all this stuff.

Finally, the porpoise started moving further north. As they increased, more and more of them would have to spread out to get more territory to accommodate the numbers. I started to have the porpoise trouble, and one day at the dock, after the porpoise beat me up, Tommy said, "See! And you'd never believe me back there when I used to tell you that the porpoise were taking my fish." Because I never went to the south end, and in the beginning, that's where they all were.

MARINELAND RELEASES

One theory is that thirteen porpoise were released from Sea World or Marineland into the Fort Pierce area thirty or forty years ago. Part of the thought is that it was because they're used to being fed by people. When we see them come up to the boat and do the tail walking and the flips, which is just what they do in Marineland and Sea World, you think, they have got to be part of those trained porpoise. Whether it is true or not, I don't know, but it leads you to believe that. They had trained them in shows. I don't remember the year it started, but they released those back to the sea down here, I'm pretty sure right here off of Fort Pierce. This is just my theory.

RECENT YEARS

Approximately fifteen years ago, '95, when the governments started regulating gear types, such as the drift nets became outlawed, number one, right around that time, the state banned net fishing in the rivers and along the beaches. It changes fishing pressures and gear types where we went from strictly in the inlet waters and the rivers, a net-type fishery, to a more hook-and-line fishery.

After the nets were gone, I adapted then to jack fishing in the Indian River Lagoon. Jack crevalles, that is, yellow-tailed jacks, as some people call them, to Spanish mackerel fishing along the beaches. Without the nets the overall production was lower, so the price was better. We could get a price where it was lucrative for us to troll these fish and make money.

As far as fishing in the river or going kingfishing, in a sense, I would rather do this. And it took some pressure off of the kingfish, where a number of us would fish jacks and Spanish mackerel and back off on putting pressure on the kingfish. And those that wanted to catch kingfish would still be kingfishing. But it made us more diversified.

So government regulations and changing of gear-type regulations, basically, it moves fishing pressures around on different species. Jacks and Spanish mackerel used to be primarily caught by gill nets. That was the primary method of fishing for them prior to the Florida net ban. Now the primary methods are just hook and line, and then they learned how to use the cast net on the Spanish mackerel and sometimes on jacks and some other fish.

But there's a very good cast-net industry now on the mackerel. And you can still net fish outside of three miles. In recent years, the kingfishing has been kind of slow in Fort Pierce in April and November. So more of us do the mackerel fishing on the beach, or the jack fishing in the river.

QUOTAS

The only quota that has affected me is on the king mackerel. We got 1,070,000 pounds that we're allowed to catch on what is called the Eastern Gulf Group Quota, from November 1 through March 31, which is what we call our winter stock of fish, where we start off on fifty head per boat. As of February 1, we go to seventy-five head per boat, till we either fill the quota or March 31 comes. That's per day, per trip. You're allowed one trip a day. If you have three-quarters or more of the quota filled, come February 1, then you just stay on fifty head till you fill the quota.

Now, come April 1, we're on the South Atlantic Quota. The South Atlantic Quota is seventy-five head per day, from the Flagler County line to Miami. That quota is roughly three million pounds. The jurisdiction range for this three million pounds is actually from North Carolina to Miami. There are different trip limits north of Flagler County.

TAGGING PROGRAMS

The National Marine Fisheries Service started the tagging program to study the stocks of fish as they migrated up and down the coast and out into the Gulf. They do some testing of the fry, the young juvenile fish, in the ocean. They have a little type seine method in which they capture the fry and determine X number per X number of drag; they do this with a seine net. They determine the species over the course of the years as to how many they should get in that given area if the stock is healthy.

The tagging and the fry, the dragging and catching the fry and the count, is called the "biomass test." That's what they do to determine the health of the fishery. These programs determine that X number of our fish in the wintertime came around the Keys, from the Gulf, and would wander up this way as far as the Cape. So that's why we have a separate quota in the wintertime of fish that still travel back and forth from the Gulf side to here.

POLLUTION

When we have real rainy periods, and because of all the drainage throughout the state and the Kissimmee River chain piping it all out to the ocean, there's no natural filtering process. It used to flow down through Okeechobee and through the Everglades, and it would filter the water much better by the time it went through all the grass and the marshes, and when the water reached the ocean, it would be much purer and cleaner.

Today, with all the canals that pump everything straight to the ocean, there's no filtering process involved. All the impurities from fertilizers and whatever is being sprayed on the land for pesticides go straight to the ocean. During heavier rainy periods, we have more sediment in the water and more problems getting clear water inshore to fish.

This is one of the reasons why I think in the last year and a half or so we've had more kingfish inshore, closer to the beach, because we have been through a drought period. There has been a lot less runoff and sediment brought from the interior of Florida to the ocean. Therefore, in the inland waters the water stays clearer. The sediment on the bottom is less. The divers will say this. It's been cleaned out, and the hurricanes helped to clean it out some, too. Today, we have less runoff coming from inland and have far less sediment on the bottom. Therefore, there's not as much stuff stirring up in the water and clouding the water up. Because of drought conditions and less freshwater runoff, it's healthier for the whole marine environment to not have the sediment.

That sediment settles from all that runoff, and the impurities settle on top of the live coral, the rocks, and just chokes them out. Today, I think even some divers will tell you the reefs are even looking better than they had been, to some degree, because there's more sunlight, and the water is clearer. The more sunlight that can get down there, the better.

ECONOMICALLY AND ENVIRONMENTALLY SOUND

I've always believed that the method we use—one line, one hook, trolling up in the water column—is environmentally wise to the ocean, the bottom, and the reefs. We don't hurt coral and don't do any bottom destruction whatsoever. And as far as the species of fish, I would say 99 percent or more of the fish we catch are still perfectly alive and healthy. If we released them, every one of them would live.

So when we catch something that we can't keep, or it's too small, or it's a sailfish, or whatever, we let it go. It has a 99.9 percent survival rate. I've always believed the hand-line trolling industry is the most environmentally friendly fishery there is. Hook-and-line fishing would never fish the fish out.

I was fishing back in the '70s, when you'd mark black wads of kingfish for five miles. When they bite, you just pull as hard as you can.

When they quit biting, the fish still mark on your recorder, and the black wads are still there, but they get just a little tighter in the middle of the range of your paper. Sometimes you can hardly get a bite. Once in a while you can catch one. When the fish feed, they feed, and when they don't, you're not going to catch them. That's it. It's environmentally friendly.

I don't believe you would ever catch out kingfish hand-line fishing. By having a hand-line fishery, you support so many more people in the workforce and in the fishery, because you're catching fish spread over a longer period of time and will average a better price. More people can be involved in it for a longer period of time. There are areas in the industry where you're going to go out and catch them all in one big gulp in one week or two weeks, and then you're done the rest of the year.

I believe that our method of hand-line fishing is the most viable fishery, economically and environmentally, that there is. There's a lot of money being put back into the economy and helping other small businesses. Look at everything that we buy, from the tackle, to the electronics, to the boat, the hauling out of the boats to repair the bottom. If you had a fishery where you had five boats, then you'd have five recorders, five radios, and five boats to haul. From Palm Beach to the Cape, we're probably buying 300 recorders and 300 radios and hauled out about twice a year, so we're adding a lot more back to the economic side of the industry, to the business side of it. It's just the most economically and environmentally sound way to fish.

FRIENDSHIPS

Over the years, I had connections with the different people, like Glenn Cameron on the *Floridian*. For several years there, I went sport fishing with him. Sometimes when he had charters or just family stuff, we'd go out and just play around, and I learned a lot from him about live-baiting. We did things together which were enjoyable. Glenn and I have a good history together, and I enjoyed those times with Glenn learning another angle of catching kingfish. I never live-baited before until I went with Glenn. I didn't know the live-bait part of it. When growing up, we used the ballyhoo and the mullet rigs, but I'd never done the live bait with the cigar minnows until I went with Glenn. We had some good times back then, the parties and friends. All those things are part of the camaraderie. Fishermen would come from up and down the coast to our Halloween parties.

There's a camaraderie you build up with your fellow fishermen, especially with your user group, because you're fishing with those people all the time. You're traveling together to where the fish are. And a lot of times, your life depends on your buddy and the boat that is out there in the area where you are. Sometimes these relationships will vary a little bit. But, basically, we all are friends with one another, and we're there to help each other if we get in trouble, which has happened to a number of us on the ocean. Then there's just regular breakdowns where you get towed in or you tow someone else.

THE *BIG CHIEF* SAVED MY LIFE

I wasn't sure when I got out of the army, not having any real education, what I was going to do. I did not have a direction in my life, and I didn't, for the long term, know how I was going to make my living or make a career. The net fishing was all right, but for me that was not big money. I knew I wanted to get a kingfish boat somehow.

Nick Kurusis first gave me the opportunity to run his boat. Then B. C. Davis gave me the opportunity to buy his brother's boat. Each one of these sequences happened a couple years apart. Then I got the opportunity to buy the *Big Chief* from Herman Summerlin, and I'm still with it today. That's basically how I got started. I put a lot of time at it. In the early years, I put many hours on that ocean.

Conclusion

The Decline of the King Mackerel Populations

The great black wads of fish that Captains George Kaul and Tris Colket once marked on their recorders are gone. The days of catching over 1,000 pounds of kingfish in a day are past. Lack of limits and the practice of overfishing with large gill nets and spotter planes in the 1970s and early 1980s contributed to the decline in the fish population. Commercial captain Roger Farlow once told me that in 1975 the circle gill nets slaughtered well over a million pounds of kingfish in two weeks north of 12A Buoy. He said no fishery can survive an onslaught like that.

When spotter planes and circle nets were outlawed for king mackerel fishing, long-drift gill nets took their place. Some were many miles long. For several years during the late 1980s, they swept the Fort Pierce waters clean. Hook-and-line troll boats had to travel many miles out of their way to navigate around these drift nets in order to access the offshore fishing grounds, only to find those grounds barren.

Then in the 1990s, purse seines began rounding up thousands of pounds of baitfish from the inshore reefs east of Fort Pierce. Commercial captain Bob Ferber said when he first came here in 1992, the piles of bait marked so thick on his recorder that he thought they were reefs or rocks on the bottom. He said that for a while those bait nets unloaded thirty to forty pounds of goggle-eye bait a day.

In addition to purse seines, the nutrient-rich and chemical runoff from industrial and agricultural interests flows from Lake Okeechobee and the interior of South Florida via canals and rivers into the Indian River Lagoon and then into the Atlantic Ocean, doing further damage to sea life.

The summers of 2011 and 2012 were the worst that I have ever seen for commercial king mackerel fishing off of the east coast of Florida. King mackerel catches in the eastern Gulf of Mexico are down, too. Today, fishermen are concerned about the residual effects of the 2010 BP Gulf of Mexico oil spill and subsequent toxic dispersant spraying on the Atlantic fishery. The Gulf Stream flows from the Gulf of Mexico around South Florida and up the state's east coast. Lately, too, fishermen are becoming suspicious of cold-water upwellings believed to be caused by arctic warming and thawing glaciers.

Perhaps the most dramatic indicator that the local east coast Florida hook-and-line troll boat commercial kingfish industry is in trouble occurred on August 18, 2011, when Captain George Kaul sold his boat, the *Big Chief*. He has given up commercial fishing for good because he believes it is no longer viable. Now, George, who has probably caught more fish than any other captain in this book, catches bass and bluegill to release into his pond, which is teeming with many kinds of Florida freshwater fish. He enjoys feeding and watching them. Since selling the *Big Chief*, George has converted a 20-foot Lester Revels–built saltwater-flats boat into a glass-bottom boat so he, his grandchildren, and friends can better observe the activities of the fish in his pond.

One can only hope and wish that this downward spiral of fish catches is a passing cycle and that, with the ocean's resilience and sound environmental and fishery management, the once-great Florida king mackerel populations will someday return.

Killing Fish

Captain Ron Lane once said to me, "Don't saltwater catfish have just as much right to live as a sailfish or marlin, or any other fish, for that matter?" He has a valid point. Commercial and charter captains prefer not to kill any fish unless they are to be used for food or bait. They certainly have no desire to kill every fish in the sea.

I am often moved by the bloody death throes of a fish at my feet in the kill box or by catching and watching fish die while packed tightly together in that hostile foreign environment. It's humbling to remember that when a fish is struggling and pulling on the line, he is fighting for his very life.

Fishermen, like farmers and ranchers, provide food. Though most are sensitive to the lives they take, the food chain is brutal, and captains are still proud of big catches.

Glossary

Bug line. A feathered hook tied to 200–300 feet of piano wire attached with a swivel to a heavy piece of monofilament line tied to an electric reel. The switch for the reel is located in the stern work area of the boat so the fisherman can easily pull the fish to the boat. The fisherman pulls or jerks this line continually to attract fish. Also called jerk bug or jerk line. Also see **Swivel**.

Dead- or live-bait sail. Sailfish caught with either dead or live bait. Fishing for sailfish, or any fish, with live bait is generally the most effective method of attracting larger predator fish. Trolling dead baits is usually not as effective. Sometimes, however, fish bite trolled dead baits, spoon lures, or lures better than they do live baits. Also see **Spoon lure**.

Drone spoon. A spoon lure used primarily for trolling. It is not as thick or heavy as a surf-casting spoon. Number 2 and #2½ Drone spoons are popular for catching Spanish mackerel; #3½ and #4 Drones are popular for king mackerel. Also see **Spoon lure**.

Fishery. All of the fish of a specific species, e.g., the pompano fishery in the Gulf of Mexico. Sometimes the term refers to more than one species or a group of species lumped together, e.g., the snapper/grouper fishery.

Fish house. A wholesale fish dealer that buys fish directly from fishermen and sells them to restaurants, retail fish markets, and other buyers. Florida fish houses often ship truckloads of fresh fish to buyers at Fulton Fish Market in New York City. Fish houses allow their fishermen to charge fuel, ice, and tackle and deduct these expenses from the fishermen's weekly paychecks.

Float line. When, instead of tying a jerk bug on the bug line, the fisherman hooks a strip bait on two hooks behind a sea witch to this same line. The fisherman does not jerk the float line; it trolls or drags freely nearer the surface, thus the name. Also see **Bug line; Sea witch**.

Gaff. A length of handle attached to a large, smooth metal hook sharpened on the end that is used to hook or land a fish into the boat. The dead weight of a large fish will often break the line if it is lifted by the line; thus the gaff is used to lift the large fish over the boat's gunwale. Flying gaffs have extra-long handles and are used mostly on charter or sports fishing vessels to hook or gaff a fish that is farther away from the stern.

Gangion. A length of line that connects a buoy to a main line. It is used in most types of longline fishing. See **Longline fishing**.

Hook-and-liner. A commercial fishermen who trolls for Spanish and king mackerel using hooks and hand lines and lands fish one at a time, by hand. Also called troll boats, hand-line kingfishermen, and hand liners.

Jig. A lure that is lifted and dropped vertically, creating a motion that attracts fish. Jigs come in many sizes, shapes, and colors. The diamond jig is a popular kingfish jig.

Kill box. A fiberglass or wooden box mounted on the deck at the commercial fisherman's workstation in the stern of the boat. An H-shaped stainless steel bar is mounted on the back of the kill box. When a fish is pulled into the boat, the fisherman slides the hooks across the center of the H, and the fish drops off the hooks and into the kill box, where it dies.

Lapstrake boat. A boat with layered planks from stem to stern. Each plank is layered over, or overlaps, the one below it. The overlapping ridges, or laps, help stabilize the boat in seas and act as small spray rails that help keep the boat and crew dry.

Live bottom. Ocean bottom that has live coral formations or wrecks or other structures that support crustaceans, small baitfish, and other sea creatures that attract and support larger predator fish.

Longline fishing. A commercial fishing technique that uses a long line, called the main line, with baited hooks attached at intervals by means of branch lines called leaders. Lines connecting the main line to buoys are called gangions.

Marker. A 100-pound-plus swordfish. A double marker is 200 pounds plus; a triple marker is 300 pounds plus; and so forth.

Paravane. See **Planer**.

Planer. Lead and stainless steel devices used to troll baits below the ocean surface. The depth they reach depends on their weight and size, the length of cable used to attach the planer to the boat outriggers, and the trolling speed of the boat. When a planer is set, it plows through the water at about a 45-degree angle with the lead hanging down. When a fish bites on the line attached to the back of the set planer, it releases the planer, which then rises to the surface, allowing the fisherman to more easily pull the fish to the boat. Also called a paravane.

Purse seine. A common type of commercial net. A line referred to as a purse line passes through rings along the bottom of the net and, when pulled, draws the rings close to one another, preventing the fish from "sounding," or diving to escape the net. It is similar to a traditional-style purse, which has a drawstring. The purse seine is preferred for capturing fish species that school close to the surface, such as sardines, mackerel, anchovies, herring, certain species of tuna, and salmon before they swim up rivers and streams to spawn. Boats equipped with purse seines are called purse seiners.

Sea witch. A longtime favorite lure for kingfish and other types of game fish such as dolphin (mahimahi), wahoo, grouper, sailfish, and marlin. For kingfish they are baited with a strip bait put on two hooks behind the sea witch. The lures are made with painted lead heads and straight nylon hair and are hand tied with stainless wire. They are available in many colors and sizes, but most kingfishermen make their own.

Spoon lure. An oblong concave metal lure with a shiny chrome or painted finish that resembles an ordinary spoon with a single or treble hook on the end. The spoon lure is mainly used to attract fish by reflecting light and moving randomly. Thicker, heavier spoon lures with treble hooks are more for casting than trolling.

Spring line. A pivot line used in docking and undocking or to prevent a boat from moving forward or astern while made fast to a dock.

Stinger rig. A lure or bait that has a trailing hook or hooks.

Sweet stack. More than one teaser bait on a single line, in tandem, one behind the other. Used in charter fishing.

Swivel. A brass or stainless steel tool that comes in many sizes and provides a strong connection between the main line and the leader to eliminate line twist. A swivel may include a snap clip on one end, in which case it is called a snap swivel.

Umbrella rig. A popular commercial king mackerel lure. Small spoons or hooks are embedded inside colored surgical tubing and tied to swivels located at the ends of the four "umbrella" bars. This type of rig can be dangerous because while one or more live fish is gyrating on it, the free hooks gyrate as well and can easily catch the fisherman's arm. Also see **Spoon lure**.

Weed line. A rough or irregular line of floating *Sargassum* seaweed that may stretch for miles. Predator fish often feed on smaller baitfish that follow these weed lines. Trolling along weed lines is a popular method to fish for dolphin (mahimahi).

Acknowledgments

My friend, neighbor, and avid angler Jan Bals kindly read and helped edit this book. Her wise and enthusiastic guidance was invaluable.

Jo Chapman of St. Augustine, Florida, added further polish and formatted the work into a presentable manuscript.

My neighbors Lynn Summerlin and Herman Summerlin and retired marine biologist Dale S. Beaumariage of Golden, Colorado, kindly shared the photos of Ray Perez's shark fishing exploits from the 1960s.

The drawing of Ray Perez's boat, the *Grand Cru,* is the work of my friend Don Clark.

Thanks to local author and historian Jean Ellen Wilson for carefully proofreading the book.

And thanks to all of the talented folks at the University Press of Florida for having faith in me and expertly guiding this work to fruition.

Finally, the extraordinary lives led by the five captains interviewed and their kind and generous willingness to share their stories made this book possible.

About the Author

Terry L. Howard was born in Indianapolis, Indiana. His childhood was divided between the city and his grandparents' farm near Wabash, Indiana, where he fished in nearby lakes and ponds. After graduating from Wittenberg University in Springfield, Ohio, he traveled to Seattle, Washington, and worked for a season salmon fishing on a commercial purse-seine vessel from Puget Sound to Alaska.

Later, Mr. Howard settled in Fort Pierce, Florida, where he taught history and geography in the St. Lucie County Public School System and fished commercially during summers, on weekends, and over holiday breaks. In 2009, after thirty-six years, he retired from teaching and now fishes full time and writes.

He and his wife Fannie raised two children, who live nearby in South Florida, and they have one grandchild. Soon, if all goes well, they'll have two grandchildren. This is Mr. Howard's second book about Atlantic fishing captains.

Artist Julie Lounibos's painting of the author's boat, *Miss Fannie,* in the Indian River Lagoon near Saint Lucie Village.

Index

Page numbers in italics refer to illustrations.

Adventurers, 9

Albinson, Jack, 13, 75

Amberjack, 6, 48, 53–54, 67, 115

Atlantic fishing captains, 1

Atlantic Group, king mackerel, 4

Aurora, 31, 143, 153

Bait: chum as, 140, 142; in commercial hook-and-line fishing, 2; in kingfishing, 48; shark, 94–95

Barracuda, 3, 5, 11, 72, 152

Baywood Fish House, *98, 99, 100, 101*

Behavior, fish, 3

Bethel Shoals Buoy, 7

Big Chief, 139–40, 154–55, *155*, 162, 178

Bite, fish or shark, 36–37, 70

Blackwelder, Dwight, 71–72

Bluefin tuna, 124–25

Bluefish, 3, 26, 84

Boat: Brown's *Playboy*, 62–63; Brown's *Second Wind*, 56, 68, 71, 81; bugs on, 169; Cameron's early, 118–19; Cameron's *Breakwater, Floridian,* and *Zeus*, 109, *111, 116,* 116–17, *117,* 123, 130; charter, *19,* 45–46, 61, 115; Colket's first, 11–12, 13; commercial hook-and-line fishing and layout of, 2–3; fire, 44–45, 171; ghosts on, 71; *Isolde*, 16–17, *17, 39*; Kaul's *Big Chief* and *Aurora*, 139–40, 153–55, *155,* 162, 178; *Last Mango, 10, 19,* 44–46, 52–53; *Miss Fannie, x, 188*; of Perez, 95–98, *96, 102, 103, 105*; Perez spotting empty, 105; sinking, 71, 131–32, 162–63; storm and impact on, 20–24, 69, 123, 162–64; wayward, 167–68

Bodies, dead, 134

Bonito, 3, 5, 94

Bottom-fishing, 67–69

Breakwater, 123, 130

Breig, Frankie, 13, 29, 31

Breig, Terry, 31

Brotherhood, commercial fishermen, 81–82

Brown, A. J.: biggest catch and fish size for, 69–70; boat sinking involving, 71; on bottom-fishing, 67–69; on catfish, 57–58; on commercial fishing compared to charters, 61; as commercial kingfisherman, 55, 61, 62; danger and injury for, 66–67, 77–80; on diving and fishing, 72–73; on diving tragedy, 71–72; on drug smuggling, 75; early fishing experience of, 55–56, 57–58; falling overboard, 77–80; family background and talents of, 55–57, 58; on fishing future, 80–81; on ghosts and UFOs, 70–71; on grouper trolling, 76–77; Horton for, 82, *82*; jetty hit by, 66–67; on kingfishing, 62, 80; on lightning storms, 74–75; on mackerel of largest size, 67; on net fishing impact on kingfishing, 63–64; as pipe-fitter, 61, 64; *Playboy* as boat of, 62–63; on rambling, 60–61; *Second Wind* boat of, *56, 68, 71, 81*; on sextant use, 66; at St. Lucie Nuclear Plant, 61–62; storms and bad weather experienced by, 64–66; on trout fishing, 74; in Vietnam, 58–60; on war, 59; warbird story of, 75; waterspout experiences of, 64–65; on wreck discovery and fishing, 68–69

Bugs, 78n2, 169

Cameron, Glenn: background and talents of, 109, 111–12; on big fish, 126, 127–28; bodies found by, 134; *Breakwater, Floridian,* and *Zeus* as boats of, 109, *110, 111, 116,* 116–17, *117,* 123, 130; canoe fishing for, 113–15; as charter captain, 45–46, 109, 135–36, *136*; charter fishing for, 112–13, 115; charter

Cameron, Glenn—*continued*
fishing mates of, *117*, 117–18, 117n1; on
commercial kingfishermen, 134–35; on
deep kingfishing, 129; dredge developed
by, 119–20; early boats of, 118–19; early
fishing experience of, 112; on first big marlin, 126–27; Kaul's friendship with, 177–78;
on lightning strikes, 124; mentors for,
119–20; on message bottles, 133; rescues
by, 129–32; on rips, 128–29; sea school
education of, 113; Smith billfishing tournament duo with, 111; on sneakerheads, 134;
storms and bad weather for, 122–24; surfing by, 113; on tournaments, 119, 120–22;
on tuna catches and Gulf Stream, 124–26
Canoe fishing, 113–15
Captains. *See* Brown, A. J.; Cameron, Glenn;
Colket, Tris; Kaul, George; Perez, Ray
Casey, Jack, 25
Castro, Fidel, 86–88
Castro, Jose, 35, 43
Catch: big fish mechanics of, 126, 127–28;
bluefin tuna, 124–25; Brown on biggest,
69–70; in canoe fishing, 113–14; Colket's
biggest kingfishing, 33; for Kaul, 155–56,
166; location for biggest, 69–70; TAC
and, 4
Catfish, 57–58, 180
Charter and charter fishing: amberjack,
53–54, *54*; boats for, *19*, 45–46, 61, 115;
for Cameron, 112–13, 115; changes in, 115;
clients in, 54; Colket on, 51–54; commercial fishing compared to, 1–2, 51–52, 61;
dolphin fishing, 46–47; fish types caught
on, 5–6; kingfishing, 48–49; mates, *117*,
117–18, 117n1, *118*; money, 115; ocean, 1–2;
smuggling and, 133–34
Charter captain: Cameron as, 45–46, 109,
135–36, *136*; client wishes for, 5; Colket on
being, 45–46; Fort Pierce as central base
for, 6; as species sustainability proponent,
8; success for, 6; talents and skills of, 5. *See
also* Cameron, Glenn; Colket, Tris
Chum, 140, 142
Clients, 5, 54
Coast Guard, 30, 31
Cobia, 3, 5, 113, 114, 166
Cojimar, Cuba, 83, 85–86, 100

Colket, Tris, 179; adventurers in family of,
9; background and nature of, 9, 10–11;
biggest kingfish catch by, 33; as charter
captain, 45–46; on charter fishing, 51–54;
comedy from, 32; on commercial fishing
and family stress, 51–52, *52*; commercial fishing early experience of, 12–13;
dangers faced by, 14–25, 30–31; dolphin
fishing for, 46–47; early fishing experience of, 10–12; education, 12; first boat
of, 11–12, 13; fog and waterspouts for,
15–18; on grouper, 50, *51*; *Isolde* of, 16–17,
17, *39*; on kingfishing, 25–26, 33, 48–49;
kingfishing co-workers of, 29; Langfitt as
fishing friend of, 12–13; *Last Mango* boat
of, *10*, *19*, 44–46, 52–53; on *Last Mango*
restoration and family bonding, 52–53;
on natural resource conservation, 40,
43–44; Ponce Inlet rescue involvement
of, 29–31; on sand tiger and great white
sharks, 37–40, *39*, *40*; on shark bite,
36–37; on shark fishing, 33–44, *37*, *39*,
40, *43*; shark-tagging by, 43–44; storms
and bad weather for, 18–25; on sunfish
or mola mola, 49–50; on swordfishing,
26–29, *27*; talent of, 13; travel range of,
31–32; on U-Hauling fish, 31–32; Vero
Beach and early experience of, 11–12
Combat, Vietnam, 145, 147–48
Comedy and humor, 32, 106, 135
Commercial fishermen: brotherhood of,
81–82; EEZ for hand-line, 8; Fort Pierce as
central base for, 6; income for, 5; Kaul as,
137, 153–54, 168; licensing for, 4–5; success
for, 6; talents of, 5. *See also* Kingfishermen, commercial
Commercial fishing: charter fishing compared to, 1–2, 51–52, 61; Colket's early
experience in, 12–13; ecological soundness
of troll kingfish in hand-line, 7–8; family
stress from, 51–52, *52*, 82; fish population
decline impact on, 179–80; Kaul on, 143,
153–54, 168; long hours in, 168; personal
responsibility in, 20; tuna, 125
Commercial hook-and-line fishing: boat layout, 2–3; equipment used in, 2; fish types
caught in, 3–4; mechanics of and dangers
in, 2–3, *4*; ocean charter fishing compared

to, 1–2; planers and line used in, 2–3. *See also* Kingfishermen, commercial

Cuba: big marlin in, 104; rafts from, 85, 85n1, 132; refugees fleeing, 88–90; revolution and counterrevolution in, 83, 86–88

Danger: Brown on injury and, 66–67, 77–80; for Colket, 14–25, 30–31; in commercial hook-and-line fishing, 2; diving, 71–72, 73–74, 130–31; fish bite, 70; from fog, 15; Fort Pierce and Sebastian Inlet, 14, 15, 65, 129–30; lightning strike, 16, 124; overboard, falling, 77–80, 123–24, 131–32; Ponce Inlet rescue, 30–31; shark bite, 36–37; waterspout, 15–18, 64–65, 69, 104, 122, 164. *See also* Storms and bad weather

Daytona, Florida, 65–66, 77

Decision-making, storm, 20, 21–22, 24

Discovery, 35–36, 68

Diving and divers: danger, 71–72, 73–74, 130–31; fishing and, 72–74; rescue involving, 130–31; tragedy involving, 71–72

Dolphin (mahimahi), 3, 5, 46–47, 49, 95, 122, 126, 132, 185

Dolphin fishing, 46–47

Dredge, 119–20

Dressing out, sharks, *34*, 34–35

Drift, 160

Drugs, 45, 75, 133–34

Easy Money, 89

Ecology, 7–8. *See also* Environment and conservation

Education: Cameron's sea school, 113; for Colket, 12; for Kaul, 143–44

EEZ. *See* Exclusive Economic Zone

Environment and conservation: fishing, economics, and, 176–77; natural resource, 40, 43–44; shark, 40, 43–44

Equipment: in commercial hook-and-line fishing, 2; kingfishing, 33, 33n3; regulation of, 174; swordfishing, 27–28, 156–57, 158–59. *See also* Bait; Line

Exclusive Economic Zone (EEZ), 4, 8

Family: Brown's, 55–57; Colket's *Last Mango* restoration and bond with, 52–53; commercial fishing and stress on, 51–52, *52*,

82; Kaul's, *138*, *140*, 153–54, 164–65, *165*; Perez's, 83–84, *84*, 88, 89, 91

Farlow, Roger, 170–71, 179

Fear, 67; in going overboard, 78, 79; during Ponce Inlet rescue, 30; in storms, 21, 22–23, 25, 64

Ferber, Bob, 68, 179

Fire, boat, 44–45, 171

Fish: behavior of, 3; Brown's biggest size of, 70; catching big, mechanics of, 126, 127–28; charters and types of, 5–6; commercial fishing impacted from population decline of, 179–80; commercial hook-and-line types of, 3–4; danger in bite of, 70; Florida and Perez's biggest, 104–5; kingfisherman identification of, 3–4; net fishing impact on population of, 179; NMFS tagging programs for, 175; purpose in killing, 180–81; U-Hauling, 31–32. *See also specific types*

Fishing: bottom-, 67–69; Brown's early experience of, 55–56, 57–58; Cameron's early experience of, 112; canoe, 113–15; Colket's early experience of, 10–12; diving and, 72–74; environmentally and economically sound, 176–77; Fort Pierce as capital of, 1; future of, 80–81, 106–7; grouper, 171–72; jerk-bug, 170–71, *171*; Kaul's early experience of, 139–40, *140–42*; lightning strikes and, 16, 65–66; light sticks used in, 156–57; longline, 85, 85n2; North Florida conditions for, 18–20; off Daytona, 77; for Perez, 108; river, 174; Sebastian Inlet as location for, 7, 31, 65; in storms, 160–61; telephone, 58; trout, 74; UFO spotted while, 70–71; in Vero Beach, 11–12; in Vietnam, 151; waterspouts and, 15–16; winter, 31; wrecks, 68–69. *See also* Charter and charter fishing; Commercial fishing; Kingfishing; Net fishing; Swordfish; Swordfishing

Flanagan, Mike, *41*, *42*

Floridian, 109, 111, *116*, 116–17, 177

Fog, 15

Fort Pierce, Florida: charter captains and commercial fishermen in, 6; dangers of inlet in, 14; as fishing capital, 1; Gulf Stream near, 6; Kaul on, 142–43, 172; offshore bar, 6–7; Perez and estate in, *107*, 107–8; porpoise in, 172; "Yankee" fishing crowd in, 13

Friendship, 177–78
Future, fishing, 80–81, 106–7

Gear. *See* Equipment
Ghosts, 71
Gilmore, Grant, 38–39, 43
Grading, swordfish, 28n2
Grand Cru, *103*, *105*
Great white sharks: Colket on, 38–40, *39*, *40*; immature or juvenile, 38–39; location for, 38
Grouper, 5, 6, 48, 51–53, 68, 80–81, 95, 98, 115, 151, 183; Kaul on fishing for, 171–72; large size, 50, *51*; trolling, 76–77
Gulf Group, king mackerel, 4
Gulf Stream, 15, 17, 18, 85n1, 89, 100, 122, 128–29, 132, 156, 161–63, 180; drift and, 160; flow of, 6; swordfish following, 157–58; Tuna across, 125–26
Guns, shark fishing, 35, 95

Hammerhead shark, 35, 40–41, *41*
Harpoon, 157
Harrison, Everett, 26–27
Harrison, Jerry, 15, 64–65
Hayes, Gene, 14
Hemingway, Ernest, 85–86
Hodges, Bill, 62
Horton, Dan, 90, 91, 92
Horton, Sherry, 82, *82*

Identification, fish, 3–4
Immigration, U.S., 89
Income. *See* Money and income
Injury, 66–67
Isolde, 16–17, *17*, *39*

Jerk-bug fishing, *170*, 170–71
Jetty, 66–67
Jones, Tommy, 63–64, 67–68, 69, 70–72, 76, 82
Jupiter, Florida, 65, 164–65

Kaul, George, 33, 179; background, personality, and talents of, 137, 139, 150; *Big Chief* and *Aurora* as boats of, 139–40, 153–55, *155*, 162, 178; biggest fish for, 166–67; bugs on boat of, 169; Cameron's friendship with, 177–78; catch for, 155–56, 166; on chum bait, 140, 142; as commercial fisherman, 137, 153–54, 168; on commercial fishing, 143, 153–54, 168; early fishing experience of, 139–40, *140–42*; education for, 143–44; on environment and economically sound fishing, 176–77; family of, *138*, *140*, 153–54, 164–65, *165*; on fishing in Vietnam, 151; on Fort Pierce, 142–43, 172; on grouper fishing, 171–72; jerk-bug fishing for, *170*, 170–71; Jupiter for, 164–65; kingfishing for, 169–70; lightning and waterspout experiences of, 164; logbook for, 155–56; on NMFS tagging programs, 175; North Carolina legal trouble for, 151–53; in Panama Canal Zone, 150; on pollution, 175–76; porpoise experience of, 172–74; purple heart for, 147–48; on radio, 137, 139; on regulation and quotas, 174–75; on shark fishing, 159–60; on storms and bad weather, 160–64, 167; swordfishing, 156–59, 167; Vietnam experience of, 144–49, 151; Wahoo for, 166
Kaul, Loretta, 137, *138*, 164, 169, 185
Killer, Ed, 111
Kingfishermen, commercial: Brown as, 55, 61, 62; Cameron on, 134–35; examples, 31; fish identification by, 3–4; heyday for, 25–26; Kaul as, 137; NMFS regulations concerning, 4; travel range for, 31–32, 63–64
Kingfishing: bait used in, 48; Breig's as world travelers in, 31; Brown on, 62, 80; charters, 48–49; Colket on, 25–26, 33, 48–49; Colket's co-workers in, 29; in deep, 129; equipment, 33, 33n3; heyday for, 25–26; for Kaul, 169–70; Kaul and biggest catch in, 166; mechanics of, 48–49; net fishing impact on, 26, 26n1, 63–64; for Perez, 98–99; pollution impact on, 176; porpoise impact on, 172, *173*; size in, 48
King mackerel, 1–3, 5–6, 9, 26, 55, 64, 67, 72–73, 78, 123, 137, 155, 174, *181*; Atlantic and Gulf Group identification, 4; ecological soundness in fishing of, 7–8; population decline, 179–80; TAC for groups of, 4
Kite, 132, 132n2
Kremmin, Warren, 53–54

Lane, Ron, 120, 129, 134, 135, 180
Langfitt, John, 12–13
Last Mango: as charter boat, *19*, 45–46;
  Colket family bond over, 52–53; Colket's
  boat, *10*, *19*, 44–46, 52–53; fire on, 44–45;
  major storm experienced in, 18, 23
Licensing and regulation: commercial hook-
  and-line fishing, 4–5; of equipment, 174;
  net fishing, 174, 179; NMFS commercial
  kingfishermen, 4; quotas and, 174–75
Life jacket. *See* Safety and safety measures,
  storm
Lightning: danger from, 16, 124; fishing and,
  16, 65–66; Perez on, 102; storms, 74–75,
  122, 124, 164
Light sticks, 156–57
Line: for commercial hook-and-line fishing,
  2–3; hand-pulled, 28–29; North Florida
  fishing conditions and, 18–20; swordfish-
  ing, 27–28, 158–59
Little George, 61
Location: biggest catch, 69–70; great white
  shark, 38; Sebastian inlet as fishing, 7, 31,
  65; shark fishing, 95; swordfish, 29
Logbook, 155–56
Long-drift gill net, 179
Longline fishing, 85, 85n2
LORAN (Long Range Navigation), 14, 15, 18
Lowe, Charlie, 31
Lowe, Steve, 31, 70, 73, 81, 101, 143

Mackerel, 67. *See also* King mackerel
Maloney, Tom, 100
Marineland, 173–74
Market, 34, 36, 41–43, 45, 91–94
Marlin, 5, 83, 85, 88, 104, 105, 126–27, 180
Masters, Larry, 89–90
Mates, charter fishing, *117*, 117–18, 117n1, *118*
McHale, Tommy, 69, 173
McManus, Brant, 158, 159, 160, 161
Mentors, 119–20
Message bottles, 133
Mine sweeping, 144–45, 146
Miss Fannie, *x*, *188*
Money and income: in charter fishing, 115;
  for commercial fishermen, 5; in sword-
  fishing, 158
Monster Hole, 14, 15, 130
Muller, Jimmy, 12

National Marine Fisheries Services (NMFS):
  commercial kingfishermen regulations
  from, 4; fish tagging programs of, 175;
  shark-tagging program involving, 25,
  43–44; species protection from, 40
Natural resources, 40, 43–44
Net fishing: fish population impact from,
  179; kingfishing impact from, 1n26, 26,
  63–64; long-drift gill, 179; regulation, 174,
  179; spotter planes used in, 26
New England, swordfishing, 157–59
NMFS. *See* National Marine Fisheries
  Services
North Carolina, 151–53

Ocean charter fishing, 1–2
Offshore bar, Fort Pierce, 6–7
Old Man and the Sea, The (Hemingway),
  85–86
Overboard, falling, 77–80, 123–24, 131–32

Panama Canal Zone, 150
Paul, Brian, 132
Paul, Kevin, 109, *117*, 117–18, 117n1
Pelican Yacht Club Sailfish Tournament,
  120–21
People, charter fishing, 54
Perez, Ray: background and talents of, 83,
  85; boat of, 95–98, *96*, *102*, *103*, *105*; on
  commercial swordfishing, 99–101, *103*; on
  Cuba and fleeing refugees, 88–90; empty
  boats spotted by, 105; family of, 83–84, *84*,
  88, 89, 91; on fishing future, 106–7; fishing
  to, 108; Florida and biggest fish of, 104–5;
  on Florida racial discrimination, 90–91;
  Fort Pierce estate of, *107*, 107–8; humorous
  stories from, 106; immigration experience
  for, 89; kingfishing for, 98–99; on lightning,
  102; on marlin in Cuba, 104; on *The Old
  Man and the Sea*, 85–86; on porpoise, 106;
  as revolutionary and counterrevolutionary, 83, 86–88; revolution disillusionment
  of, 87–88; shark fishing involvement of,
  90, 91–98, *93–94*, *96*; on storms and bad
  weather, 102; on submarine missile shots,
  105–6; U.S. crossing for, 88–89
Personal responsibility, 20
Physical conditions, storm, 20–21, 22–23, 65,
  122–23, 162–64

Pipe-fitter, 61, 64
Planers, 2
Playboy, 62–63
Pollution, 175–76
Ponce Inlet: Coast Guard and rescue at, 30, 31; Colket and rescue at, 29–31; danger during rescue at, 30–31; evolution of, 29–30; fear during rescue in, 30
Population, king mackerel, 179–80
Porpoise, 2, 94–95, 107–8, 127; in Fort Pierce, 172; history, 173; kingfishing impact from, 172, 173; Perez on, 106; Sea World and Marineland releases of, 173–74
Presidential Palace, Cuban, 86–87
Protected species, 40. *See also* Environment and conservation
Purple heart, 147–48
Purpose, killing with, 180–81
Putnam, Dave, 90, 91, 92

Quotas, 174–75

Racial discrimination, 90–91
Radio: Kaul on, 137, 139; in storms, 21–22; VHF, 21
Rafts, Cuban, 85, 85n1, 132
Rambling, 60–61
Reeves, Jimmy, 66, 71, 81
Refugees, Cuban, 88–90
Regulation. *See* Licensing and regulation
Rescue: by Cameron, 129–32; Colket on Ponce Inlet, 29–31; diver, 130–31; at Sebastian Inlet, 131–32
Responsibility. *See* Personal responsibility
Revolution and counterrevolution, Cuban: disillusionment with, 87–88; Perez in, 83, 86–88; presidential palace attack in, 86–87
Rips, 128–29
River fishing, 174

Safety and safety measures, storm, 20–21, 23
Sailfish, 5, 111, 119–20, 140–42, 153, 176, 180
Sand tiger shark, *37*, 37–38
Santes, Anselmo ("Chief"), 92, *93*, 94, *94*, 106
Schorner, Jeff, 73–74
Sea World: porpoise released from, 173–74; sand tiger shark and, *37*, 37–38; sunfish for, 49–50

Sebastian Inlet: dangers of, 14, 15, 65, 129–30; as fishing location, 7, 31, 65; fog in, 15; Monster Hole of, 14, 15; rescue at, 131–32; winter fishing in, 31
Second Wind, *56*, *68*, *71*, *81*
Selling. *See* Market
Sextant, 66
Shafer, Chip, 119–20
Sharks and shark fishing: bait for, 94–95; bite, 36–37; Colket on, 33–44, *37*, *39*, *40*, *43*; conservation, 40, 43–44; discovery of species in, 35–36; dressing out, *34*, 34–35; experts on, 35, 38–39, 43; great white, 38–40, *39*, *40*; guns for, 35, 95; hammerhead, 40–41, *41*; Kaul on, 159–60; location, 95; market for, 34, 36, 41–43, 91–94; mechanics of, 36, 92–94, 159; NMFS program for tagging, 25, 43–44; Perez involved in, 90, 91–98, *93*–*94*, *96*; sand tiger, *37*, 37–38; size of, 35, 38–39, 40–41, 95–96; skinning and processing, 91, 92–95, *93*–*94*, *97*, 159; tagging of, 25, 43–44; tiger, 35, *42*, 42–43, 44, 95–96; types, 35–36
Sinking, boat, 71, 131–32, 162–63
Size: Brown's fish of biggest, 70; in dolphin fishing, 46–47; grouper of large, 50, *51*; in kingfishing, 48; mackerel and largest, 67; marlin, 104; shark, 35, 38–39, 40–41, 95–96; swordfish, 28–29, 28n2
SKA. *See* Southern Atlantic Kingfish Association
Skinning and processing, shark, 91, 92–95, *93*–*94*, *97*, 159
Smith, Sandy, 109, 111
Smuggling, 75, 133–34
Snapper, red, 5–6, 61, 70–73, 98, 115, 129, 151, 183
Sneakerheads (remora), 134
Snook, 11, 61, 74
Southern Atlantic Kingfish Association (SKA), 109, 111
Spanish mackerel, 3, 8, 26, 139, 174, 183
Species and species sustainability, 8, 35–36, 40. *See also* Environment and conservation
Spotter planes, 26, 179
St. Lucie Nuclear Plant, 61–62
Storms and bad weather: boat impact from, 20, 22–24, 69, 123, 162–64; Brown's experi-

ence of, 64–66; Cameron on bad weather and, 122–24; Colket's experience of major, 18–25; decision-making in, 20, 21–22, 24; fear during, 21, 22–23, 25, 64; fishing in, 160–61; freak waves in, 167; Jupiter and Daytona, 65–66; Kaul on, 160–64, 167; lightning, 74–75, 122, 124, 164; for Perez, 102; physical conditions during, 20–21, 22–23, 65, 122–23, 162–64; radio in, 21–22; rips, 128–29; safety measures in major, 20–21, 23
Submarine, 105–6
Success, 6
Summerlin, Herman, *101*, 143, 154
Sunfish or mola mola, 49–50, *50*
Surfing, 113
Swanson, Mike, *41, 42*
Swordfish, 18, 20, 26–30, 34, 85, 88, 99–103, 156–57, 167, 184
Swordfishing: Colket on, 26–29, *27*; equipment, 27–28, 156–57, 158–59; grading in, 28n2; Gulf Stream for, 157–58; harpoon use in, 157; heyday for, 27–28; by Kaul, 156–59, 167; line for, 27–28, 158–59; location, 29; money in, 158; New England, 157–59; Perez on commercial, 99–101, *103*; size, 28–29, 28n2; triple marker, *28*

TAC. *See* Total allowable catch
Talents: of Brown, 55; of Cameron, 109; of charter captains, 5; of Colket, 13; of commercial fishermen, 5; of Kaul, 137
Tanker, hitting, 75
Telephone fishing, 58
Tiger shark, *42*; market for, 42–43; size, 35, 95–96; travel range of, 44
Total allowable catch (TAC), 4
Tournaments, 111, 119, 120–22
Tragedy, diving, 71–72

Travel, 31–32, 44, 63–64
Trolling, 76–77
Trout, 74
Tuna, 3, 31, 85, 104–5, 109, 122, 139, 161–62, 185; bluefin catches, 124–25; commercial fishing for, 125; Gulf Stream, 125–26
Tyrrell, Al, 16, 31–32, 65n1

UFO (unidentified flying object), 70–71
U-Hauling, 31–32
United States (U.S.): immigration into, 89; Perez on crossing to, 88–89; Vietnam and treatment in returning to, 60

Vero Beach, Florida, 11–12
VHF (Very High Frequency), 21
Vietnam: Brown in, 58–60; cave killers in, 60; combat in, 145, 147–48; fishing in, 151; Kaul's experience in, 144–49, 151; latrine duty in, 149; mine sweeping in, 144–45, 146; perimeter breach in, 148–49; surviving in, 146–47; training for, 144; U.S. treatment after, 60

Wahoo, 3, 5, 49, 70, 113, 166, 185
War, 59. *See also* Vietnam
Warbird, 75
Waterspouts: as danger, 15–18, 64–65, 69, 104, 122, 164; double, 15–16, *16*; fishing and, 15–16
Weather. *See* Storms and bad weather
Wells, Lewis, 29, 31–32
Winter, fishing, 31
Wrecks, 68–69

"Yankee" fishing crowd, 13

Zeus, 109–11
Zodiac, 132

WILD FLORIDA

Edited by M. Timothy O'Keefe

Books in this series are written for the many people who visit and/or move to Florida to participate in our remarkable outdoors, an environment rich in birds, animals, and activities, many exclusive to this state. Books in the series will offer readers a variety of formats: natural history guides, historical outdoor guides, guides to some of Florida's most popular pastimes and activities, and memoirs of outdoors folk and their unique lifestyles.

30 Eco-Trips in Florida: The Best Nature Excursions (and How to Leave Only Your Footprints), by Holly Ambrose (2005)

Hiker's Guide to the Sunshine State, by Sandra Friend (2005)

Fishing Florida's Flats: A Guide to Bonefish, Tarpon, Permit, and Much More, by Jan S. Maizler (2007)

50 Great Walks in Florida, by Lucy Beebe Tobias (2008)

Hiking the Florida Trail: 1,100 Miles, 78 Days, Two Pairs of Boots, and One Heck of an Adventure, by Johnny Molloy (2008)

The Complete Florida Beach Guide, by Mary and Bill Burnham (2008)

The Saltwater Angler's Guide to Florida's Big Bend and Emerald Coast, by Tommy L. Thompson (2009)

Secrets from Florida's Master Anglers, by Ron Presley (2009)

Exploring Florida's Botanical Wonders: A Guide to Ancient Trees, Unique Flora, and Wildflower Walks, by Sandra Friend (2010)

Florida's Fishing Legends and Pioneers, by Doug Kelly (2011)

Fishing Secrets from Florida's East Coast, by Ron Presley (2012)

The Saltwater Angler's Guide to Tampa Bay and Florida's West Coast, by Tommy L. Thompson (2012)

High Seas Wranglers: The Lives of Atlantic Fishing Captains, by Terry L. Howard (2013)